Large Language Models Graph RAG

A Hands-On Guide to Knowledge Graph Integration with LLMs

©

Written By

Morgan Devline

Copyright Page

Large Language Models Graph RAG: A Hands-On Guide to Knowledge Graph Integration with LLMs
Copyright © 2024 by Morgan Devline.
All rights reserved.

For additional resources, updates, and supplementary materials related to this book, visit:
[Morgan Devline Collection on Amazon]

Dedication:
To those who believe in the power of knowledge to transform the world.

Table of content

Preface

Motivation for Writing the Book

Artificial Intelligence (AI) has evolved dramatically over the past decade, with Large Language Models (LLMs) emerging as a cornerstone of this evolution. These models, powered by advanced architectures like transformers, have revolutionized how machines understand and generate human language. However, while their potential is vast, LLMs face challenges—notably their reliance on static datasets and susceptibility to generating inaccurate or contextually irrelevant responses.

This is where **Graph Retrieval-Augmented Generation (Graph RAG)** comes into play. By integrating knowledge graphs into the workflow of LLMs, we can overcome many of these limitations. Knowledge graphs offer a structured, relational representation of data, allowing LLMs to perform context-aware reasoning and deliver precise, well-grounded responses. This book is born out of the need to bridge the gap between theory and practice, empowering AI practitioners to harness the combined power of LLMs and knowledge graphs.

I wrote this book with three key goals in mind:

1. **Practicality**: Provide readers with actionable knowledge to implement Graph RAG in real-world applications.

2. **Accessibility**: Break down complex concepts into digestible, easy-to-understand explanations.

3. **Relevance**: Cover the latest advancements in Graph RAG, ensuring the content reflects cutting-edge practices and tools.

I believe that integrating knowledge graphs with LLMs represents a paradigm shift in AI, enabling smarter, more efficient systems. Whether you are a developer, researcher, or AI enthusiast, this book will equip you with the tools and insights needed to succeed in this exciting field.

Who This Book is For

This book is designed for a wide range of audiences, from beginners to experienced professionals. Here's a breakdown of who can benefit:

1. **AI Developers and Engineers**:

   o If you are building applications powered by LLMs and want to enhance their accuracy and contextual understanding, this book provides step-by-step guidance on integrating knowledge graphs into your workflows.

2. **Data Scientists**:

   o For those working with large datasets and looking to create or manage knowledge graphs, this book covers essential tools, frameworks, and methodologies.

3. **Researchers**:

   o If you are exploring the frontiers of AI and want to understand the theoretical underpinnings of Graph RAG, this book dives deep into the concepts and includes references to foundational and cutting-edge research papers.

4. **Students and Enthusiasts**:

   o This book provides foundational knowledge and practical exercises, making it an excellent resource for anyone new to AI or looking to expand their skill set in graph-based systems.

5. **Industry Professionals**:

   o For product managers, business analysts, or decision-makers, the book's real-world case studies and application examples demonstrate how Graph RAG can solve industry-specific challenges.

How to Use This Book

This book is structured to accommodate readers at various levels of expertise. Whether you prefer to follow the chapters sequentially or jump to specific sections, the book is designed to be flexible and intuitive.

Chapter Overview

1. **Foundational Concepts**:

   o Chapters 1 through 4 introduce Large Language Models, Graph RAG, and knowledge graphs. These chapters are ideal for readers new to the topics or those looking to solidify their foundational knowledge.

2. **Hands-On Implementation**:

   o Chapters 5 through 8 focus on practical applications, with detailed instructions, code examples, and tools to help you build and deploy Graph RAG systems.

3. **Advanced Topics**:

   o Chapters 9 and 10 delve into scaling, optimization, and cutting-edge applications of Graph RAG in domains like healthcare, e-commerce, and legal research.

4. **Ethical and Practical Considerations**:

   o Chapter 11 explores challenges, ethical concerns, and best practices, ensuring that your implementations are responsible and effective.

5. **Case Studies and Future Directions**:

   o Chapters 12 through 15 include real-world examples, industry case studies, and predictions for the future of

Graph RAG, offering inspiration and strategic insights.

Interactive Learning Features

- **Code Examples**: Each chapter includes complete, well-commented code snippets to demonstrate key concepts. For example, you will learn how to query a knowledge graph using SPARQL and integrate the results into an LLM pipeline.

- **Practice Problems**: Exercises at the end of each chapter help reinforce learning. These problems range from beginner-friendly tasks to advanced challenges, ensuring a hands-on experience.

- **Companion Resources**: A dedicated GitHub repository accompanies this book, containing all the code examples, datasets, and templates you'll need to follow along.

- **Visual Aids**: Diagrams, flowcharts, and screenshots provide additional clarity, helping you visualize complex workflows and systems.

Advanced Reader's Path (Guide to Advanced Topics)

For readers already familiar with the basics of LLMs, knowledge graphs, and Graph RAG, the advanced chapters offer in-depth exploration of topics such as:

- **Dynamic Knowledge Graph Updates**: Learn how to handle real-time changes in graph data.

- **Scaling Graph Retrieval**: Techniques for managing large-scale graphs with billions of nodes and edges.

- **Graph Neural Networks (GNNs)**: Integrate GNNs for enhanced reasoning and prediction.

- **Cross-Domain Applications**: Explore how Graph RAG can be applied across healthcare, finance, and more.

These sections are clearly marked, so advanced readers can dive directly into the most relevant material.

Tips for Getting the Most Out of This Book

1. **Follow Along with Code**:

    o Set up your development environment early (Chapter 5 provides detailed guidance) and execute the provided examples as you progress.

2. **Experiment and Innovate**:

    o Use the practice problems and case studies as a springboard to experiment with your own ideas and applications.

3. **Stay Curious**:

    o The final chapters include suggestions for further reading and exploration, encouraging you to stay engaged with the latest advancements in Graph RAG.

Acknowledgments

This book is the result of collaboration, hard work, and inspiration from many individuals. I would like to extend our heartfelt gratitude to:

- **The AI Community**: For their groundbreaking research and tools that laid the foundation for Graph RAG.

- **My Reviewers**: For providing invaluable feedback to ensure the accuracy and quality of the content.

- **My Readers**: Your curiosity and drive to learn are the true motivation behind this book.

- **My Family and Friends**: For their unwavering support and encouragement throughout this journey.

I hope this book inspires you as much as the journey of writing it inspired me.

Chapter 1: Introduction to Large Language Models and Graph RAG

1.1 What Are Large Language Models (LLMs)?

Large Language Models (LLMs) are advanced machine learning models designed to understand, generate, and manipulate human language. They are based on deep learning architectures, particularly transformers, which enable them to process vast amounts of textual data and learn intricate patterns in language. Examples of LLMs include OpenAI's GPT series, Google's BERT, and Meta's LLaMA models.

Key Features of LLMs

1. **Scale**: LLMs are trained on massive datasets, often containing billions of words sourced from books, websites, and other digital content.

2. **Context Awareness**: They use attention mechanisms to understand the context of words within a sentence or paragraph, enabling coherent and meaningful responses.

3. **Generalization**: LLMs are capable of performing a wide variety of language tasks, such as translation, summarization, question answering, and content generation, often without task-specific fine-tuning.

4. **Adaptability**: With fine-tuning or prompting, LLMs can specialize in domain-specific applications, such as medical diagnosis or legal document analysis.

How LLMs Work

LLMs leverage the **transformer architecture**, a neural network structure that uses attention mechanisms to weigh the importance of different words in a sentence. This allows them to process language bidirectionally and generate predictions for the next word or phrase based on prior input.

Benefits and Limitations

Benefits	Limitations
Highly versatile across tasks	Susceptible to generating false or biased information
Handles complex contexts well	Computationally expensive
Improves with fine-tuning	Requires massive datasets
Easy to deploy via APIs	Struggles with reasoning tasks

Code Example: Basic Use of an LLM

Here's a simple Python example using OpenAI's GPT API to generate a response:

```python
import openai


# Set up API key
openai.api_key = "your-api-key"

# Define a prompt
prompt = "Explain the significance of Large Language Models."

# Generate a response
response = openai.Completion.create(
    engine="text-davinci-003",
    prompt=prompt,
    max_tokens=100
)

# Print the result
print(response.choices[0].text.strip())
```

This code sends a prompt to an LLM and prints the generated response, showcasing how easily LLMs can process and respond to queries.

1.2 Retrieval-Augmented Generation (RAG): An Overview

Retrieval-Augmented Generation (RAG) is a paradigm that combines the generative capabilities of LLMs with the retrieval power of external knowledge sources. Instead of relying solely on the LLM's internal data, RAG pipelines fetch relevant information from external databases or documents to enhance accuracy and relevance.

How RAG Works

1. **Query Generation**: The user's input or question is sent to the retrieval module.

2. **Information Retrieval**: Relevant documents or knowledge pieces are retrieved from an external source, such as a database or a knowledge graph.

3. **Answer Generation**: The retrieved information is combined with the LLM's generative capabilities to produce a final response.

Key Advantages of RAG

1. **Up-to-Date Information**: By leveraging external sources, RAG can provide answers based on the latest data, overcoming the static nature of LLM training.

2. **Reduced Hallucinations**: Retrieval ensures that responses are grounded in factual data.

3. **Domain-Specific Accuracy**: By retrieving domain-specific information, RAG improves the precision of specialized tasks.

RAG Architecture

The RAG workflow typically includes:

1. **Retriever**: A module (e.g., Elasticsearch, FAISS) that retrieves relevant documents based on the input query.

2. **Generator**: An LLM that generates the response by integrating retrieved data.

Code Example: Basic RAG Workflow

Below is a simplified implementation of a RAG system using Python:

```python
from transformers import pipeline


# Load a retrieval model
retriever = pipeline("document-question-answering",
model="deepset/roberta-base-squad2")

# Sample documents
documents = [
    "Large Language Models are AI systems that process and generate human language.",
    "Retrieval-Augmented Generation enhances LLMs with external knowledge sources."
]

# User query
query = "What is RAG?"

# Retrieve the most relevant document
result = retriever(question=query, context=" ".join(documents))
print("Answer:", result['answer'])
```

This example shows how retrieval can augment the generative process by fetching specific information from external sources.

1.3 Graph RAG: Enhancing RAG with Knowledge Graphs

Graph RAG takes the RAG framework to the next level by integrating **knowledge graphs** as the retrieval mechanism. Unlike traditional retrieval systems, knowledge graphs represent information as interconnected nodes and edges, capturing relationships and context in a structured format.

Why Use Knowledge Graphs in RAG?

1. **Structured Context**: Knowledge graphs provide relational data, allowing the LLM to reason over connections between entities.

2. **Enhanced Accuracy**: Graphs can represent domain-specific knowledge with precision, reducing ambiguity.

3. **Explainability**: Responses derived from graphs can be traced back to their source nodes and relationships, ensuring transparency.

How Graph RAG Works

1. **Graph Querying**: The retriever interacts with the knowledge graph using query languages like SPARQL or Cypher.

2. **Context Generation**: Retrieved graph data is formatted and sent to the LLM as contextual input.

3. **Answer Generation**: The LLM integrates graph-derived context to generate an enriched response.

Code Example: Querying a Knowledge Graph

Here's an example using Neo4j to query a knowledge graph:

from neo4j import GraphDatabase

```python
# Connect to Neo4j database
driver = GraphDatabase.driver("bolt://localhost:7687", auth=("neo4j",
"password"))

# Define a query
query = """
MATCH (n:Entity)-[r:RELATION]->(m:Entity)
WHERE n.name = $entity_name
RETURN m.name AS related_entity
"""

# Execute the query
def query_graph(entity_name):
    with driver.session() as session:
        result = session.run(query, entity_name=entity_name)
        return [record["related_entity"] for record in result]

# Fetch related entities
related_entities = query_graph("Graph RAG")
print("Related entities:", related_entities)
```

This example demonstrates how to retrieve related entities from a knowledge graph to augment the LLM's input.

Summary

- **LLMs** excel in understanding and generating language but face limitations in reasoning and dynamic knowledge updates.

- **RAG** addresses these limitations by integrating retrieval mechanisms, improving factual accuracy and domain specificity.

- **Graph RAG** further enhances RAG by leveraging structured knowledge graphs, enabling contextual reasoning and explainability.

Together, these technologies represent a transformative approach to building smarter, more reliable AI systems. The following chapters will delve deeper into the practical implementation and applications of Graph RAG.

1.4 Why Knowledge Graph Integration Matters

Knowledge graph integration is a transformative step in advancing AI systems by addressing several critical limitations of traditional retrieval and generative mechanisms. Integrating knowledge graphs with Retrieval-Augmented Generation (RAG) enables structured, contextualized, and explainable responses, which are increasingly vital for complex problem-solving.

1.4.1 Structured Representation of Knowledge

Knowledge graphs store information in a structured manner, using nodes to represent entities (e.g., people, places, concepts) and edges to denote relationships between these entities. This organization provides a highly interpretable framework for:

- **Understanding Context**: Knowledge graphs capture the nuances of relationships, enabling more meaningful and accurate answers.

- **Multi-Hop Reasoning**: Unlike flat databases, knowledge graphs can represent multi-layered relationships, allowing systems to deduce indirect connections.

1.4.2 Enhanced Reasoning Capabilities

Knowledge graphs amplify the reasoning capabilities of AI by offering explicit relationships that LLMs can process effectively. For instance:

- **Example**: In a medical context, a query about a symptom like "cough" can traverse a knowledge graph to identify related diseases, treatments, and medications, delivering a more comprehensive response.

1.4.3 Explainability and Traceability

One of the major challenges in AI is explainability—users need to trust and understand how an answer was generated. Knowledge graphs offer:

- **Traceable Sources**: Each node and edge in a graph can link back to its source data, ensuring transparency.

- **Explainable Outputs**: Systems can explain their reasoning process by citing relationships and pathways within the graph.

1.4.4 Scalability and Flexibility

Knowledge graphs can be scaled to incorporate vast amounts of domain-specific data. They are also flexible, allowing updates and modifications without requiring extensive retraining of the underlying AI model.

- **Example**: A financial knowledge graph can be updated with new market trends or regulations, keeping the AI system relevant and accurate.

1.5 Real-World Applications of Graph RAG

Graph RAG has applications across numerous industries, where structured knowledge and contextual understanding are critical. Below are some key domains:

1.5.1 Healthcare

- **Use Case**: Assisting in diagnosis and treatment planning.

- **Example**: A healthcare knowledge graph connects symptoms to diseases, treatments, and medications. For instance, given the input "fever and cough," the system can retrieve connections to potential diagnoses such as influenza or COVID-19 and recommend treatments.

1.5.2 Legal Research

- **Use Case**: Streamlining legal document retrieval and analysis.

- **Example**: A legal knowledge graph containing case law, statutes, and legal precedents enables LLMs to trace relationships between legal concepts, significantly reducing research time.

1.5.3 E-Commerce

- **Use Case**: Delivering personalized product recommendations.

- **Example**: Graph RAG links user preferences with product attributes and purchase histories. For a customer searching for "laptops," the system could suggest accessories, warranties, or similar products based on the graph's connections.

1.5.4 Scientific Research

- **Use Case**: Discovering novel insights by analyzing research papers.

- **Example**: A knowledge graph derived from scientific literature can connect methodologies, results, and citations, helping researchers identify unexplored areas or related studies.

1.5.5 Conversational AI

- **Use Case**: Providing contextually accurate and dynamic responses.

- **Example**: A customer service chatbot augmented with a domain-specific knowledge graph (e.g., for banking) can provide detailed, accurate answers about account details, transactions, and policies.

1.6 Comparing RAG and Graph RAG

To better understand the difference between RAG and Graph RAG, consider the following :

Description

Feature	RAG	Graph RAG
Data Source	Flat databases, document repositories	Knowledge graphs with structured nodes and edges
Retrieval Mechanism	Text-based search	Graph traversal using queries (e.g., SPARQL, Cypher)
Context Generation	Retrieved text chunks	Retrieved entities and relationships
Reasoning Capability	Limited to retrieved text	Multi-hop reasoning over graph connections
Explainability	Minimal	High, with traceable relationships and pathways
Examples of Usage	FAQ systems, general search engines	Complex problem-solving, domain-specific applications

Illustrative Diagram

Below is a visual representation comparing the workflows of RAG and Graph RAG:

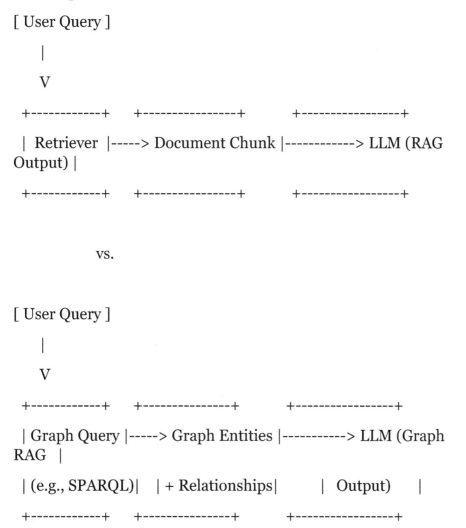

```
[ User Query ]

    |

    V

  +------------+    +----------------+        +----------------+

  | Retriever  |-----> Document Chunk |------------> LLM (RAG
  Output) |

  +------------+    +----------------+        +----------------+


             vs.


[ User Query ]

    |

    V

  +------------+    +---------------+        +----------------+

  | Graph Query |-----> Graph Entities |-----------> LLM (Graph
  RAG  |

  | (e.g., SPARQL)|   | + Relationships|        | Output)     |

  +------------+    +---------------+        +----------------+
```

This diagram highlights how Graph RAG builds on traditional RAG by incorporating structured graph data, enabling deeper reasoning and more precise responses.

Summary

- Knowledge graph integration enhances AI systems by providing structured, explainable, and scalable knowledge.

- Real-world applications of Graph RAG span industries such as healthcare, legal research, e-commerce, scientific discovery, and conversational AI.

- Comparing RAG and Graph RAG reveals the latter's advantages in reasoning and explainability, making it a powerful tool for domain-specific tasks.

Chapter 2: Foundations of Large Language Models

2.1 Understanding the Architecture of LLMs

Large Language Models (LLMs) are advanced neural network-based systems designed to process and generate human language. They are built upon the **transformer architecture**, which enables them to capture relationships between words and their contexts, even across long sequences of text.

2.1.1 Key Components of LLMs

1. **Input Embeddings**:

   o Converts words, phrases, or tokens into numerical vectors that can be processed by the model.

   o Similar words or tokens are mapped close to each other in this vector space.

   o Example: The words *king* and *queen* might have similar embeddings due to their semantic similarity.

2. **Positional Encodings**:

   o Preserves the order of words in a sequence since transformers process all words simultaneously (non-sequentially).

   o Adds unique information to embeddings to help the model understand the sentence structure.

3. **Self-Attention Mechanism**:

   o Assigns importance to different words in a sequence relative to each other.

- Example: In the sentence, "The cat sat on the mat," the model determines that *cat* and *sat* are closely related.

4. **Multi-Head Attention**:

   - Enhances the self-attention mechanism by running multiple attention calculations in parallel.

   - Captures various aspects of relationships within the sequence.

5. **Feedforward Neural Networks**:

   - Further processes contextual embeddings derived from attention mechanisms.

   - Applies transformations to refine the representations.

6. **Output Layer**:

   - Produces predictions such as the next word in a sentence or classification results.

   - Example: Predicting *"mat"* as the next word in "The cat sat on the ...."

2.2 Transformer Models: A Primer

The **transformer model**, introduced in the groundbreaking paper *"Attention Is All You Need"* (Vaswani et al., 2017), is the backbone of modern LLMs like GPT and BERT. It replaced sequential models such as RNNs and LSTMs by enabling parallel processing and better handling of long-range dependencies in text.

2.2.1 Core Components of a Transformer

Component	Purpose
Input Embedding Layer	Converts tokens into high-dimensional vectors.
Positional Encoding	Adds information about word order.

Component	Purpose
Self-Attention Mechanism	Identifies important parts of the input sequence.
Multi-Head Attention	Performs multiple attention calculations for diverse insights.
Feedforward Network	Processes contextual embeddings for better representation.
Layer Normalization	Stabilizes and speeds up training.
Output Layer	Generates predictions or final outputs.

2.2.2 Attention Mechanisms

Transformers rely heavily on attention mechanisms, which calculate how much focus each word in the input should receive.

- **Self-Attention**: Each word is compared to every other word to determine relationships.

    o Example: In the question, *"What did Einstein discover?"*, self-attention links *Einstein* with *discover* to focus on relevant information.

- **Multi-Head Attention**: Splits the self-attention process into multiple "heads," allowing the model to capture various patterns or relationships within the data.

2.2.3 Advantages of Transformers

1. **Parallelization**: Processes input sequences simultaneously rather than one step at a time, speeding up training and inference.

2. **Handling Long Contexts**: Captures dependencies over long sequences effectively, outperforming RNNs and LSTMs.

3. **Scalability**: Enables training larger models with billions of parameters, as seen in GPT-3 and BERT.

Code Example: Using a Transformer for Sentiment Analysis

python

```
from transformers import pipeline

# Load a pre-trained transformer model
sentiment_analyzer = pipeline("sentiment-analysis")

# Input text
text = "Transformers are revolutionizing natural language processing!"

# Perform sentiment analysis
result = sentiment_analyzer(text)
print(result)
```

Output:

plaintext

```
[{'label': 'POSITIVE', 'score': 0.9998}]
```

2.3 Pretraining and Fine-Tuning of LLMs

LLMs are trained in two primary phases: **pretraining** and **fine-tuning**.

2.3.1 Pretraining

- **Objective**: Teach the model to learn general language representations from large, diverse datasets.

- **How It Works**:

    o The model is exposed to tasks such as **masked language modeling (MLM)** or **causal language modeling (CLM)**.

- Example Task: Predict missing words in a sentence (MLM).
  - Input: "The cat sat on the [MASK]."
  - Output: "mat."

- **Datasets**:
  - Models are pretrained on massive datasets like Wikipedia, Common Crawl, or digitized books.

2.3.2 Fine-Tuning

- **Objective**: Adapt the pretrained model to specific tasks or domains.

- **How It Works**:
  - Fine-tuning uses smaller, task-specific datasets to refine the model's performance on a particular application.
  - Example Task: Sentiment Analysis
    - Input: "The product was fantastic."
    - Output: "Positive."

Comparison of Pretraining and Fine-Tuning

Aspect	Pretraining	Fine-Tuning
Purpose	Learn general language patterns	Adapt to specific tasks/domains
Dataset	Large, general-purpose datasets	Task-specific or domain-specific
Training Time	Longer	Shorter

Code Example: Fine-Tuning a Pretrained Transformer

python

```python
from transformers import BertTokenizer, BertForSequenceClassification
from transformers import Trainer, TrainingArguments

# Load pretrained BERT model and tokenizer
model = BertForSequenceClassification.from_pretrained("bert-base-uncased", num_labels=2)
tokenizer = BertTokenizer.from_pretrained("bert-base-uncased")

# Sample dataset
texts = ["This movie is great!", "I didn't like the meal."]
labels = [1, 0]  # 1: Positive, 0: Negative

# Tokenize inputs
inputs = tokenizer(texts, padding=True, truncation=True, return_tensors="pt")

# Define training arguments
training_args = TrainingArguments(
    output_dir="./results",
    num_train_epochs=3,
    per_device_train_batch_size=4,
    evaluation_strategy="epoch",
    save_steps=10,
    save_total_limit=2,
)

# Train the model
trainer = Trainer(
    model=model,
    args=training_args,
    train_dataset=inputs,
)
```

```
trainer.train()
```

This example fine-tunes a BERT model for sentiment analysis using a small labeled dataset.

Summary

1. **Understanding the Architecture of LLMs**: These models rely on components like embeddings, attention mechanisms, and feedforward networks to process language effectively.

2. **Transformer Models**: They have revolutionized NLP by enabling parallelization, scalability, and enhanced contextual understanding.

3. **Pretraining and Fine-Tuning**: These phases ensure LLMs are both general-purpose and adaptable to specific applications.

2.4 Limitations of LLMs Without External Knowledge

While Large Language Models (LLMs) are powerful tools capable of understanding and generating human-like text, they are not without limitations, particularly when they lack access to external, up-to-date knowledge sources. Below are some of the key limitations:

2.4.1 Static Knowledge

- **Issue**: LLMs rely on the data they were trained on, which becomes outdated over time.

- **Example**: A model trained in 2021 might not have information about events or developments from 2022 onwards.

- **Impact**: The inability to retrieve real-time knowledge limits the relevance of their responses.

2.4.2 Inaccurate or Fabricated Information

- **Issue**: When LLMs encounter gaps in their training data, they tend to generate plausible-sounding but incorrect answers, often referred to as "hallucinations."

- **Example**: Asking an LLM about niche scientific concepts it wasn't trained on may result in fabricated responses.

- **Impact**: Reduces trust and reliability in critical applications like healthcare or legal advice.

2.4.3 Context Limitations

- **Issue**: LLMs struggle with maintaining a consistent context across long conversations or documents due to token limits.

- **Example**: A 10,000-word technical document may exceed the LLM's input window, causing loss of critical information.

- **Impact**: Makes it challenging to use LLMs for tasks requiring deep analysis or summarization of lengthy content.

2.4.4 Lack of Explainability

- **Issue**: LLMs do not inherently provide justifications for their outputs.

- **Example**: If an LLM suggests a medical treatment, it cannot explain the underlying rationale.

- **Impact**: Makes it difficult to verify responses, particularly in regulated industries like finance or healthcare.

2.4.5 Difficulty in Domain-Specific Adaptation

- **Issue**: General-purpose LLMs often perform poorly in specialized domains without additional fine-tuning or external data.

- **Example**: A general model may not accurately analyze legal documents unless it is adapted to the legal domain.

- **Impact**: Limits their effectiveness in niche applications without further customization.

2.5 Bridging the Gap with Retrieval-Augmented Generation

Retrieval-Augmented Generation (RAG) addresses the limitations of LLMs by combining their generative capabilities with external retrieval systems. This approach provides real-time, accurate, and contextually enriched responses.

2.5.1 How RAG Works

RAG enhances LLMs in three key stages:

1. **Query Generation**: The LLM formulates a query from the user input.

2. **External Retrieval**: A retrieval engine fetches relevant information from external knowledge sources, such as databases, knowledge graphs, or APIs.

3. **Response Generation**: The retrieved information is combined with the LLM's reasoning capabilities to generate a well-informed response.

2.5.2 Benefits of RAG

Challenge Addressed	Solution with RAG
Static Knowledge	Real-time retrieval ensures responses include up-to-date data.
Inaccurate Information	Grounding responses in retrieved facts reduces hallucinations.
Context Limitations	Allows dynamic inclusion of additional data into the context.

Challenge Addressed	Solution with RAG
Lack of Explainability	Responses can be linked to specific retrieved documents.
Domain Adaptation	Retrieval sources can be tailored to specific domains.

2.5.3 Example: Healthcare Application

- **Scenario**: A patient queries, "What are the symptoms of the latest flu strain?"

- **RAG Process**:

    1. **LLM**: Interprets the question and generates a query for the knowledge base.

    2. **Retriever**: Fetches recent medical guidelines or articles on the latest flu strain.

    3. **LLM Output**: Combines the retrieved information to produce an accurate, context-rich answer.

2.5.4 Implementation Example: RAG Workflow

python

```
from transformers import pipeline

# Define documents to retrieve from
documents = [
    "Flu symptoms include fever, cough, and fatigue.",
    "COVID-19 symptoms include loss of taste, fever, and cough."
]

# Load a question-answering pipeline
retriever = pipeline("question-answering")

# User query
```

```
query = "What are the symptoms of flu?"

# Retrieve the most relevant document
result = retriever(question=query, context=" ".join(documents))
print("Answer:", result['answer'])
```
Output:

plaintext

Answer: fever, cough, and fatigue

2.6 Practice Problem: Analyzing Transformer Architectures

This exercise helps reinforce understanding of transformer architectures by applying theoretical knowledge to practical tasks.

Problem Statement

Given the following tasks, explain how the transformer architecture addresses them. Optionally, write Python code to implement the tasks:

1. **Task 1**: Identify the role of multi-head attention in capturing relationships between words in a sentence.

2. **Task 2**: Demonstrate how positional encodings help preserve word order.

3. **Task 3**: Modify a pre-trained transformer model to classify text into categories.

Hints and Expected Outcomes

1. **Multi-Head Attention**:

    o   Use multiple attention heads to capture different semantic relationships.

    o   Example: "Paris" in "Paris is the capital of France" is related to both "capital" and "France."

2. **Positional Encodings**:

   o Highlight how positional encoding assigns unique values to tokens based on their positions, enabling sequence understanding.

3. **Transformer Modification**:

   o Use libraries like transformers to fine-tune pre-trained models for specific tasks.

Solution Example

python

```python
from transformers import BertTokenizer, BertForSequenceClassification
from transformers import Trainer, TrainingArguments

# Task 3: Fine-tune a pre-trained transformer for text classification

# Load BERT model and tokenizer
model = BertForSequenceClassification.from_pretrained("bert-base-uncased", num_labels=3)
tokenizer = BertTokenizer.from_pretrained("bert-base-uncased")

# Sample dataset
texts = ["This is fantastic!", "I hated this experience.", "It was okay."]
labels = [0, 1, 2]  # 0: Positive, 1: Negative, 2: Neutral

# Tokenize input data
inputs = tokenizer(texts, padding=True, truncation=True, return_tensors="pt")

# Define training arguments
training_args = TrainingArguments(
    output_dir="./results",
    num_train_epochs=2,
    per_device_train_batch_size=2,
```

```
    evaluation_strategy="epoch"
)

# Train the model
trainer = Trainer(
    model=model,
    args=training_args,
    train_dataset=inputs
)

trainer.train()
```

Summary

- LLMs face significant limitations without external knowledge, including static information and a lack of explainability.

- Retrieval-Augmented Generation bridges these gaps by grounding LLMs in real-time, contextual information from external sources.

- Practice problems like analyzing transformer architectures allow learners to reinforce theoretical understanding through practical applications.

The next chapter will delve deeper into how these foundational principles enable seamless integration of knowledge graphs with RAG systems.

Chapter 3: Foundations of Graph RAG

3.1 What Makes Graph RAG Unique?

Graph Retrieval-Augmented Generation (Graph RAG) builds on the traditional RAG framework by incorporating **knowledge graphs** as the primary retrieval mechanism. Unlike conventional RAG systems that retrieve unstructured text chunks, Graph RAG leverages the structured nature of knowledge graphs to enable richer, more precise, and explainable AI outputs.

3.1.1 Key Features of Graph RAG

1. **Structured Contextual Data**:

   o Knowledge graphs organize data into nodes (entities) and edges (relationships), enabling the AI to reason about explicit connections.

   o **Example**: A knowledge graph linking "Einstein" (node) to "Theory of Relativity" (node) via "developed" (edge).

2. **Enhanced Reasoning**:

   o Graph RAG supports **multi-hop reasoning**, where the system deduces indirect connections through intermediate nodes.

   o **Example**: From "COVID-19" to "Fever" and then to "Inflammatory Response" using connected edges.

3. **Explainability and Traceability**:

   o Responses generated by Graph RAG can be traced back to specific nodes and edges, making the AI's reasoning process transparent.

- o **Example**: Explaining "Einstein developed the Theory of Relativity" by pointing to the respective nodes and relationships in the graph.

4. **Real-Time Updates**:

   - o Graphs can be dynamically updated with new data without retraining the LLM, ensuring systems remain current.

   - o **Example**: A knowledge graph for medical research can incorporate the latest findings on treatments or symptoms.

5. **Domain-Specific Accuracy**:

   - o By tailoring knowledge graphs to specific industries, Graph RAG delivers highly accurate and contextually relevant outputs.

   - o **Example**: A legal knowledge graph with case laws and statutes enhances accuracy in legal research.

3.1.2 Comparison with Traditional RAG

Feature	Traditional RAG	Graph RAG
Data Structure	Unstructured text chunks	Structured nodes and edges
Retrieval Mechanism	Text-based search	Graph traversal
Contextual Reasoning	Limited to retrieved text snippets	Multi-hop reasoning over graph data
Explainability	Minimal	High, via graph traceability
Scalability	Dependent on document indexing	Scalable with dynamic graph updates

3.2 The Role of Graph Traversal in Retrieval

Graph traversal is the process of navigating through nodes and edges in a knowledge graph to retrieve relevant information. It plays a pivotal role in Graph RAG systems by enabling targeted, efficient, and context-aware retrieval.

3.2.1 Types of Graph Traversal

1. **Depth-First Search (DFS)**:

   o Explores as far as possible along a branch before backtracking.

   o **Example**: Searching for all downstream nodes from "COVID-19" to related symptoms, then to treatment nodes.

2. **Breadth-First Search (BFS)**:

   o Explores all neighboring nodes at the current level before moving deeper.

   o **Example**: Retrieving all direct relationships for "Einstein," such as "developed," "awarded," and "published."

3. **Shortest Path Algorithms**:

   o Finds the shortest path between two nodes.

   o **Example**: Identifying the quickest connection between "Fever" and "Inflammatory Response" in a medical graph.

4. **Random Walks**:

   o Randomly traverses the graph to sample nodes, often used for probabilistic graph exploration.

   o **Example**: Sampling potential drug interactions in a pharmaceutical knowledge graph.

3.2.2 Graph Query Languages

Graph traversal is often executed using specialized query languages:

1. **Cypher (Neo4j)**:
   - Used in Neo4j databases to query nodes, edges, and relationships.
   - **Example Query**:

cypher

MATCH (person:Scientist)-[:DEVELOPED]->(theory:Theory)

WHERE person.name = "Einstein"

RETURN theory.name

Output: Theory of Relativity

2. **SPARQL**:
   - Designed for querying RDF (Resource Description Framework) data.
   - **Example Query**:

sparql

SELECT ?theory

WHERE {

 ?person rdf:type :Scientist .

 ?person :developed ?theory .

 FILTER (?person = "Einstein")

}

3. **Gremlin**:
   - Supports graph traversal in Apache TinkerPop-enabled databases.

- Example Query:

gremlin

g.V().has("name", "Einstein").out("developed").values("name")

3.2.3 Use Case: Graph Traversal in Action

Scenario: A user queries, "What is the relationship between COVID-19 and fever?"

1. **Graph Representation**:

   - Nodes: COVID-19, Fever, Inflammatory Response

   - Edges: causes, symptom of

2. **Graph Query**:

cypher

```
MATCH (disease:Disease)-[:CAUSES]->(symptom:Symptom)
WHERE disease.name = "COVID-19"
RETURN symptom.name
```

Output: Fever

3.3 Quick Start with Graph RAG: Fast-Track Implementation

This section provides a step-by-step guide to quickly implement a basic Graph RAG system using Neo4j.

3.3.1 Prerequisites

1. Install Neo4j Community Edition.

2. Set up the Neo4j Python driver:

bash

```
pip install neo4j
```

3.3.2 Setting Up the Knowledge Graph

1. **Create Nodes and Relationships**:

cypher

```cypher
CREATE (covid:Disease {name: "COVID-19"})
CREATE (fever:Symptom {name: "Fever"})
CREATE (cough:Symptom {name: "Cough"})
CREATE (covid)-[:CAUSES]->(fever)
CREATE (covid)-[:CAUSES]->(cough)
```

2. **Verify Graph Content**:

cypher

```cypher
MATCH (n)
RETURN n
```

3.3.3 Python Integration

Code Example:

python

```python
from neo4j import GraphDatabase

# Connect to Neo4j
driver = GraphDatabase.driver("bolt://localhost:7687", auth=("neo4j",
"password"))
```

```python
# Define a query function
def query_graph(disease_name):
    query = """
    MATCH (d:Disease)-[:CAUSES]->(s:Symptom)
    WHERE d.name = $name
    RETURN s.name AS symptom
    """
    with driver.session() as session:
        result = session.run(query, name=disease_name)
        return [record["symptom"] for record in result]


# Query the graph
symptoms = query_graph("COVID-19")
print("Symptoms caused by COVID-19:", symptoms)
```

Output:

plaintext

Symptoms caused by COVID-19: ['Fever', 'Cough']

3.3.4 Enhancing with LLMs

The retrieved symptoms can now be passed as context to an LLM for generating a more detailed response:

python

```python
from transformers import pipeline

# Load an LLM
generator = pipeline("text-generation", model="gpt-3.5")

# Generate a detailed response
context = "COVID-19 causes Fever and Cough."
response = generator(f"Explain: {context}", max_length=50)
print(response[0]["generated_text"])
```

Summary

- **Graph RAG Uniqueness**: Graph RAG's structured retrieval, reasoning, and explainability make it a significant upgrade from traditional RAG systems.

- **Graph Traversal**: Essential for navigating knowledge graphs, with tools like Cypher and SPARQL enabling efficient queries.

- **Quick Start**: Implementing a basic Graph RAG system with Neo4j and Python demonstrates its practical application.

3.4 Challenges in Graph-Based Retrieval

Graph-based retrieval systems bring immense value through structured data and multi-hop reasoning, but they are not without challenges. Implementing and maintaining these systems requires addressing various technical and operational hurdles.

3.4.1 Scalability

- **Problem**: As the size of a graph increases, queries become more computationally expensive, especially with dense connections and large node sets.

- **Example**: A knowledge graph with millions of nodes and edges, such as one used by Google Knowledge Graph, requires efficient storage and retrieval mechanisms.

- **Solution**: Use distributed graph databases like Neo4j AuraDB or Apache JanusGraph, and implement indexing strategies to speed up graph traversal.

3.4.2 Real-Time Updates

- **Problem**: Dynamic domains (e.g., healthcare or finance) require frequent updates to graph data without compromising system performance.

- **Example**: Adding new drug interactions to a pharmaceutical graph while ensuring existing queries remain consistent.

- **Solution**: Implement real-time update mechanisms using event-driven pipelines that synchronize new data with minimal latency.

3.4.3 Query Complexity

- **Problem**: Complex queries involving multi-hop relationships can lead to high computational overhead and slower response times.

- **Example**: Identifying diseases caused by a symptom linked through multiple intermediate conditions in a medical graph.

- **Solution**: Optimize query paths with algorithms like shortest-path traversal and use query caching to store frequently accessed results.

3.4.4 Data Integration

- **Problem**: Integrating data from disparate sources often results in inconsistencies, missing links, or redundant nodes.

- **Example**: Combining datasets from different research institutions may introduce mismatched entity labels.

- **Solution**: Use entity resolution techniques to match, merge, and standardize nodes across datasets.

3.4.5 Explainability and Traceability

- **Problem**: While knowledge graphs provide transparency, presenting the retrieved paths and relationships in an understandable format can be challenging.

- **Example**: Explaining a recommendation from a graph traversal to non-technical stakeholders.

- **Solution**: Develop user-friendly visualization tools to display graph nodes, edges, and traversal pathways.

3.5 Benefits of Graph RAG Over Traditional RAG

Graph RAG combines the structured reasoning of knowledge graphs with the generative capabilities of LLMs, addressing many limitations of traditional RAG systems.

3.5.1 Enhanced Contextual Reasoning

- **Benefit**: Graph RAG enables multi-hop reasoning by connecting multiple entities through relationships, leading to more insightful and comprehensive answers.

- **Example**: In a medical context, it can trace connections from "Fever" to "COVID-19" and then to "Viral Infection" to explain symptoms.

3.5.2 Domain-Specific Precision

- **Benefit**: Knowledge graphs tailored to specific domains (e.g., legal, healthcare) improve the accuracy of responses.

- **Example**: A legal knowledge graph with statutes, case laws, and precedents ensures precise legal answers.

3.5.3 Explainability and Trust

- **Benefit**: Graph RAG provides clear pathways for how an answer was derived, improving transparency and user trust.

- **Example**: A recommendation system can show the nodes and relationships traversed to suggest a product.

3.5.4 Dynamic Knowledge Integration

- **Benefit**: Knowledge graphs can be updated dynamically, ensuring responses remain current without retraining the LLM.

- **Example**: Adding recent research findings to a scientific knowledge graph allows for up-to-date answers.

3.5.5 Improved Scalability

- **Benefit**: Distributed graph databases and efficient query mechanisms make Graph RAG systems scalable to large datasets.

- **Example**: E-commerce platforms can manage graphs with millions of products and relationships for personalized recommendations.

Feature	Traditional RAG	Graph RAG
Data Structure	Unstructured documents	Structured nodes and relationships
Explainability	Limited	High, with clear graph traversal pathways
Reasoning Capability	Limited to retrieved snippets	Multi-hop reasoning across graph data
Real-Time Updates	Requires retraining the model	Dynamic updates without retraining
Domain Adaptation	Requires custom training for each domain	Easily adaptable via tailored knowledge graphs

3.6 Code Example: Implementing a Basic Graph Retrieval System

Below is a Python-based implementation of a basic graph retrieval system using Neo4j. This example demonstrates how to query a knowledge graph and retrieve relevant relationships.

Step 1: Setting Up Neo4j

1. Install Neo4j Community Edition or use Neo4j AuraDB (cloud-based).

2. Set up the Neo4j Python driver:

bash

pip install neo4j

Step 2: Creating a Knowledge Graph

Run the following Cypher commands in the Neo4j browser to create nodes and relationships:

cypher

```
CREATE (disease:Disease {name: "COVID-19"})

CREATE (fever:Symptom {name: "Fever"})

CREATE (cough:Symptom {name: "Cough"})

CREATE (treatment:Treatment {name: "Rest and Hydration"})

CREATE (disease)-[:CAUSES]->(fever)

CREATE (disease)-[:CAUSES]->(cough)

CREATE (disease)-[:TREATED_BY]->(treatment)
```

Step 3: Python Code for Graph Retrieval

The following Python script connects to Neo4j, queries the graph, and retrieves relevant information.

python

```
from neo4j import GraphDatabase

# Connect to Neo4j database
```

```python
driver = GraphDatabase.driver("bolt://localhost:7687", auth=("neo4j",
"password"))

# Function to query the graph
def query_graph(disease_name):
    query = """
    MATCH (d:Disease {name: $disease_name})-[:CAUSES]-
>(s:Symptom)
    RETURN s.name AS symptom
    """
    with driver.session() as session:
        result = session.run(query, disease_name=disease_name)
        symptoms = [record["symptom"] for record in result]
        return symptoms

# Query the graph for COVID-19
disease = "COVID-19"
symptoms = query_graph(disease)
print(f"Symptoms caused by {disease}: {symptoms}")
```

Output:

plaintext

Symptoms caused by COVID-19: ['Fever', 'Cough']

Step 4: Integration with LLMs

You can pass the retrieved symptoms as input context to an LLM
for generating detailed responses:

python

```python
from transformers import pipeline

# Load a pre-trained LLM
generator = pipeline("text-generation", model="gpt-3.5")
```

```
# Generate a response
context = f"COVID-19 causes the following symptoms: {',
'.join(symptoms)}."
response = generator(f"Explain: {context}", max_length=50)
print(response[0]["generated_text"])
```

Output:

plaintext

COVID-19 causes the following symptoms: Fever, Cough. These are common indicators of viral infections and may require rest and hydration.

Summary

- **Challenges in Graph-Based Retrieval**: Scalability, real-time updates, and query complexity are major hurdles, but solutions like distributed databases and query optimization mitigate these issues.

- **Benefits of Graph RAG**: It offers structured reasoning, domain-specific precision, dynamic updates, and high explainability, surpassing traditional RAG systems.

- **Implementation Example**: A step-by-step guide to setting up a basic graph retrieval system highlights how Graph RAG works in practice.

Chapter 4: Introduction to Knowledge Graphs

4.1 What Are Knowledge Graphs?

A **Knowledge Graph (KG)** is a structured representation of data that connects entities (nodes) through defined relationships (edges) to encode knowledge. Unlike flat databases, knowledge graphs are designed to capture the semantics of information, enabling AI systems to reason over interconnected data.

4.1.1 Defining Knowledge Graphs

- A knowledge graph organizes information into a graph structure where:

    o **Nodes** represent entities or concepts (e.g., "Einstein," "COVID-19").

    o **Edges** denote relationships between entities (e.g., "developed," "causes").

    o **Attributes** provide additional information about nodes or edges (e.g., a node labeled "Einstein" may have an attribute "Born: 1879").

4.1.2 Key Characteristics

1. **Semantic Context**: Captures the meaning and relationships of data, enabling contextual understanding.

2. **Interconnectivity**: Allows multi-hop reasoning by connecting related entities.

3. **Explainability**: Provides a traceable pathway for any derived knowledge.

4.1.3 Benefits of Knowledge Graphs

Feature	Benefit

Feature	Benefit
Structured Data	Organizes information for efficient querying and reasoning.
Semantic Understanding	Encodes relationships, enabling AI to infer new insights.
Explainability	Offers transparency in decision-making processes.
Dynamic Updates	Allows for real-time modifications to knowledge.

4.1.4 Real-World Examples

1. **Google Knowledge Graph**:

   - Enhances search results with rich contextual information.

   - Example: A search for "Einstein" returns facts, images, and related concepts like "Theory of Relativity."

2. **Medical Knowledge Graphs**:

   - Links diseases, symptoms, and treatments.

   - Example: Connecting "COVID-19" to "Fever" and "Hydration Therapy."

4.2 Components of a Knowledge Graph: Nodes, Edges, and Attributes

A knowledge graph's utility lies in its ability to represent and interlink diverse types of data. The three core components are:

4.2.1 Nodes

- **Definition**: Represent entities, concepts, or objects in the graph.
- **Examples**:
    - People: "Albert Einstein," "Marie Curie."
    - Places: "Paris," "Mount Everest."
    - Concepts: "Theory of Relativity," "Photosynthesis."
- **Attributes of Nodes**:
    - Metadata associated with nodes.
    - Example:
        - Node: "Einstein"
        - Attributes: {Name: Einstein, Birth Year: 1879, Field: Physics}

4.2.2 Edges

- **Definition**: Represent relationships between nodes.
- **Examples**:
    - "Einstein" → "Developed" → "Theory of Relativity."
    - "COVID-19" → "Causes" → "Fever."
- **Attributes of Edges**:
    - Can include relationship strength, duration, or confidence scores.
    - Example:
        - Edge: "Developed"
        - Attributes: {Year: 1905}

4.2.3 Attributes

- **Definition**: Properties or metadata associated with nodes or edges.
- **Examples**:

- Node Attributes: {Population: 8.9 million} for a city node like "London."

- Edge Attributes: {Confidence: 0.95} for a relationship like "Cures."

4.2.4 Visualization Example

A simple knowledge graph connecting "Einstein" to his contributions:

plaintext

```
[ Einstein ] --Developed--> [ Theory of Relativity ]

    |

  Born In

    |

  [ Germany ]
```

4.2.5 Code Example: Creating Nodes and Edges in Neo4j

cypher

```
// Create nodes
CREATE (einstein:Person {name: "Albert Einstein", born: 1879, field: "Physics"})
CREATE (relativity:Theory {name: "Theory of Relativity", year: 1905})

// Create relationships
CREATE (einstein)-[:DEVELOPED {year: 1905}]->(relativity)
CREATE (einstein)-[:BORN_IN]->(:Country {name: "Germany"})
```

4.3 Types of Knowledge Graphs

Knowledge graphs can be classified into several types based on their structure, purpose, and level of semantic complexity. Below are the key types:

4.3.1 Ontological Knowledge Graphs

- **Definition**: Capture domain-specific knowledge with a formal schema and reasoning rules.

- **Examples**:

    o **Medical Ontology**: Defines diseases, symptoms, and treatments with rules like "If symptom X and Y, then disease Z."

    o **SNOMED CT**: A widely used medical ontology.

- **Key Features**:

    o Rich semantic structure.

    o Includes axioms and constraints for reasoning.

4.3.2 Taxonomical Knowledge Graphs

- **Definition**: Represent hierarchical relationships between entities.

- **Examples**:

    o **Biological Taxonomy**: Classifies species (e.g., Kingdom → Phylum → Class).

    o **Product Taxonomy**: Categorizes e-commerce products (e.g., Electronics → Phones → Smartphones).

- **Key Features**:

    o Simple tree-like structure.

    o Limited to hierarchical relationships.

4.3.3 Heterogeneous Knowledge Graphs

- **Definition**: Combine multiple types of entities and relationships within a single graph.

- **Examples**:

  - **Social Graphs**: Link users, posts, and interactions (e.g., Facebook).

  - **Academic Graphs**: Connect papers, authors, and institutions (e.g., Semantic Scholar).

- **Key Features**:

  - Diverse entity and relationship types.

  - Supports cross-domain reasoning.

4.3.4 Knowledge Bases

- **Definition**: Simplified graphs storing factual data without deep semantics.

- **Examples**:

  - **Wikidata**: A collaborative knowledge base for open data.

- **Key Features**:

  - Focus on data storage and retrieval.

  - Limited reasoning capabilities.

Comparison Table: Types of Knowledge Graphs

Type	Structure	Key Use Cases	Examples
Ontological	Schema with rules and axioms	Complex reasoning, domain modeling	SNOMED CT, FIBO
Taxonomical	Tree-like hierarchy	Classification, categorization	Biological Taxonomy
Heterogeneous	Mixed nodes and edges	Social and academic networks	Facebook, Semantic

Type	Structure	Key Use Cases	Examples
			Scholar
Knowledge Bases	Simplified graph, limited rules	Fact storage, quick retrieval	Wikidata

4.3.5 Code Example: Building an Ontological Knowledge Graph

Below is an example of building a simple ontology for diseases and treatments:

cypher

```
CREATE (fever:Symptom {name: "Fever"})
CREATE (cough:Symptom {name: "Cough"})
CREATE (covid:Disease {name: "COVID-19"})
CREATE (hydration:Treatment {name: "Hydration Therapy"})

// Relationships
CREATE (covid)-[:HAS_SYMPTOM]->(fever)
CREATE (covid)-[:HAS_SYMPTOM]->(cough)
CREATE (covid)-[:TREATED_BY]->(hydration)
```

Summary

- **What Are Knowledge Graphs?**: They represent entities and relationships, enabling structured reasoning.

- **Components**: Nodes, edges, and attributes form the core of any knowledge graph, capturing semantic and contextual information.

- **Types of Knowledge Graphs**: Ontological, taxonomical, heterogeneous, and knowledge bases serve different purposes, from reasoning to data retrieval.

4.4 Tools and Frameworks for Building Knowledge Graphs

Building a knowledge graph requires the right tools and frameworks to efficiently create, manage, and query structured data. These tools vary in functionality, ranging from graph databases to visualization and query frameworks.

4.4.1 Graph Databases

Graph databases are the foundation for storing and querying knowledge graphs. They allow efficient traversal of nodes and edges.

1. **Neo4j**:

   o **Overview**: A popular open-source graph database optimized for connected data.

   o **Features**:

      ▪ Cypher query language for graph traversal.

      ▪ Native graph storage and processing.

      ▪ Community and enterprise editions.

   o **Use Cases**: Social networks, recommendation systems, fraud detection.

   o **Code Example**: Creating nodes and relationships in Neo4j:

cypher

```
CREATE (einstein:Person {name: "Albert Einstein"})
CREATE (relativity:Theory {name: "Theory of Relativity"})
CREATE (einstein)-[:DEVELOPED]->(relativity)
```

2. **ArangoDB**:

- o **Overview**: A multi-model database supporting graphs, documents, and key-value pairs.

- o **Features**:

  - AQL (ArangoDB Query Language) for versatile graph queries.

  - Integrated analytics and visualization.

- o **Use Cases**: E-commerce graphs, multi-modal applications.

3. **Amazon Neptune**:

- o **Overview**: A fully managed graph database service.

- o **Features**:

  - Supports multiple query languages (Gremlin, SPARQL).

  - Scalability for large datasets.

- o **Use Cases**: Recommendation engines, knowledge-based AI.

4. **JanusGraph**:

- o **Overview**: A scalable, distributed graph database optimized for handling massive graphs.

- o **Features**:

  - Integration with backends like HBase and Cassandra.

  - Apache TinkerPop framework compatibility.

- o **Use Cases**: Enterprise knowledge graphs, network analysis.

4.4.2 Query Languages

1. **Cypher** (Used in Neo4j):

- o Intuitive syntax for querying graphs.

- o Example: Finding all theories developed by Einstein:

cypher

```
MATCH (person:Person)-[:DEVELOPED]->(theory:Theory)
WHERE person.name = "Albert Einstein"
RETURN theory.name
```

2. **SPARQL:**

- o Used for querying RDF-based graphs like those in semantic web applications.

- o Example: Retrieving diseases linked to a symptom:

sparql

```
SELECT ?disease
WHERE {
  ?disease :hasSymptom :Fever .
}
```

3. **Gremlin:**

- o A graph traversal language for Apache TinkerPop-enabled systems.

- o Example: Finding all symptoms caused by COVID-19:

gremlin

```
g.V().has("name", "COVID-19").out("hasSymptom").values("name")
```

4.4.3 Visualization Tools

1. **Gephi:**

- o Open-source software for graph visualization and exploration.

- o Features include layout algorithms, clustering, and real-time exploration.

2. **Graphistry**:
   - o A GPU-powered graph visualization platform.
   - o Ideal for large-scale graphs.

3. **Neo4j Bloom**:
   - o A visualization tool tailored for Neo4j databases.
   - o Allows non-technical users to interact with graphs using natural language.

4.5 Real-World Knowledge Graph Examples

Knowledge graphs are widely used across industries, solving complex problems by connecting diverse datasets.

4.5.1 Google Knowledge Graph

- **Purpose**: Enhances Google search with structured information.
- **How It Works**:
  - o Connects entities like people, places, and concepts.
  - o Provides quick facts and related information.
- **Example**: Searching for "Albert Einstein" provides:
  - o Birth and death dates.
  - o Key contributions like "Theory of Relativity."

4.5.2 LinkedIn Economic Graph

- **Purpose**: Models the global economy by linking professionals, companies, and skills.
- **How It Works**:
  - Nodes: Users, jobs, companies.
  - Edges: Relationships like "works at," "applies to."
- **Use Cases**:
  - Personalized job recommendations.
  - Skills analysis for workforce planning.

4.5.3 Amazon Product Graph

- **Purpose**: Powers Amazon's recommendation system.
- **How It Works**:
  - Nodes: Products, categories, users.
  - Edges: Relationships like "bought together," "viewed after."
- **Use Cases**:
  - Suggesting complementary products.
  - Understanding customer preferences.

4.5.4 IBM Watson Discovery

- **Purpose**: A domain-specific knowledge graph for healthcare, finance, and legal sectors.
- **How It Works**:
  - Combines natural language processing (NLP) with structured data.
  - Links entities like diseases, treatments, and research papers.

- **Use Cases**:
  - Accelerating drug discovery.
  - Providing actionable insights in legal cases.

4.6 Diagram: Anatomy of a Knowledge Graph

The anatomy of a knowledge graph includes nodes, edges, and attributes that interconnect data. Below is a conceptual representation.

Visual Representation

plaintext

```
[ Albert Einstein ] --DEVELOPED--> [ Theory of Relativity ]

     |                    |

  BORN IN           STUDIED BY

     |                    |

 [ Germany ]       [ Modern Physicists ]
```

Explanation of Components

1. **Nodes**:
   - Represent entities like "Albert Einstein" and "Theory of Relativity."
   - Attributes can include {Name: Albert Einstein, Born: 1879} for a node.

2. **Edges**:

- Represent relationships like "DEVELOPED" and "BORN IN."

- Attributes include metadata like {Year: 1905} for the "DEVELOPED" edge.

3. **Traversal Pathways**:

- Allow navigation between nodes.

- Example: Starting at "Albert Einstein" and traversing to "Theory of Relativity" through the "DEVELOPED" relationship.

Code Example: Visualizing with Python

Using networkx and matplotlib to create and visualize a small knowledge graph:

python

```python
import networkx as nx
import matplotlib.pyplot as plt

# Create a directed graph
graph = nx.DiGraph()

# Add nodes
graph.add_node("Albert Einstein", role="Physicist")
graph.add_node("Theory of Relativity", type="Theory")
graph.add_node("Germany", type="Country")

# Add edges
graph.add_edge("Albert Einstein", "Theory of Relativity",
relation="DEVELOPED")
graph.add_edge("Albert Einstein", "Germany", relation="BORN IN")

# Visualize the graph
```

```
pos = nx.spring_layout(graph)
nx.draw(graph, pos, with_labels=True, node_size=3000,
node_color="skyblue")
nx.draw_networkx_edge_labels(graph, pos, edge_labels={
    ("Albert Einstein", "Theory of Relativity"): "DEVELOPED",
    ("Albert Einstein", "Germany"): "BORN IN"
})
plt.show()
```

Summary

1. **Tools and Frameworks**: Graph databases like Neo4j and query languages like SPARQL are essential for building and managing knowledge graphs.

2. **Real-World Applications**: Knowledge graphs power Google search, LinkedIn recommendations, and Amazon product suggestions.

3. **Diagram of Anatomy**: Knowledge graphs connect nodes and edges, enabling structured reasoning and visualization.

The next chapter will delve into designing and optimizing knowledge graphs for integration with LLMs and Graph RAG systems.

Chapter 5: Setting Up the Environment

5.1 Installing Required Tools and Libraries

To implement a Graph RAG system, you need specific tools, libraries, and platforms for creating, managing, and querying knowledge graphs and integrating them with LLMs. Below is a step-by-step guide to setting up the required environment.

5.1.1 Setting Up Python Environment

1. **Install Python**:

   o Download and install the latest version of Python from python.org.

   o Verify installation:

bash

```
python --version
```

2. **Create a Virtual Environment**:

   o Use venv or conda to manage dependencies:

bash

```
python -m venv graph_rag_env
source graph_rag_env/bin/activate  # Linux/macOS
graph_rag_env\\Scripts\\activate   # Windows
```

3. **Install Required Libraries**:

   o Common Python libraries for Graph RAG:

bash

```
pip install neo4j rdflib transformers networkx matplotlib pandas
```

5.2 Knowledge Graph Platforms

5.2.1 Neo4j

- **Overview**: A leading graph database platform that stores and queries graph data natively.

- **Installation**:

  1. Download Neo4j from neo4j.com.

  2. Start the Neo4j database server.

bash

```
./bin/neo4j start  # Linux/macOS
bin\\neo4j.bat start  # Windows
```

  3. Access the Neo4j browser at http://localhost:7474.

- **Key Features**:

  o Cypher query language for graph traversal.

  o Visualization of nodes and relationships.

  o Scalable to large datasets.

- **Connecting Neo4j with Python**: Install the Neo4j Python driver:

bash

```
pip install neo4j
Example Python code:
python

from neo4j import GraphDatabase

# Connect to Neo4j database
driver = GraphDatabase.driver("bolt://localhost:7687", auth=("neo4j",
"password"))

def query_graph():
    query = "MATCH (n) RETURN n.name"
    with driver.session() as session:
        result = session.run(query)
        for record in result:
            print(record["n.name"])

query_graph()
```

5.2.2 RDFLib

- **Overview**: A Python library for working with RDF
  (Resource Description Framework) data.

- **Installation**:

bash

```
pip install rdflib
```

- **Key Features**:

    o Create, parse, and query RDF triples.

    o SPARQL support for querying RDF graphs.

- **Code Example**: Creating and querying an RDF graph:

python

```
from rdflib import Graph, URIRef, Literal, Namespace

# Create an RDF graph
g = Graph()
ns = Namespace("http://example.org/")

# Add triples
g.add((ns["Albert_Einstein"], ns["developed"],
ns["Theory_of_Relativity"]))
g.add((ns["Albert_Einstein"], ns["born_in"], Literal("Germany")))

# Query the graph
for s, p, o in g:
    print(f"{s} {p} {o}")
```

5.2.3 Amazon Neptune

- **Overview**: A fully managed graph database service by AWS.

- **Setup**:

    o Create an Amazon Neptune cluster through the AWS Management Console.

    o Connect using Gremlin, SPARQL, or a REST API.

- **Use Cases**:

    o Large-scale knowledge graphs.

    o Integration with AWS services like SageMaker for AI workflows.

5.2.4 Apache Jena

- **Overview**: An open-source Java framework for building and querying RDF graphs.

- **Installation**:

- o Download Apache Jena from jena.apache.org.

- o Set up the Fuseki server for SPARQL queries.

- **Use Cases**:

  - o Semantic web applications.

  - o RDF data management.

5.3 Python Libraries for Graph RAG and LLMs

5.3.1 Neo4j Python Driver

- **Purpose**: Connects Python applications to Neo4j databases.

- **Key Methods**:

  - o GraphDatabase.driver: Establishes the connection.

  - o session.run: Executes Cypher queries.

- **Example**:

python

```python
def query_symptoms(disease_name):
    query = """
    MATCH (d:Disease {name: $name})-[:CAUSES]->(s:Symptom)
    RETURN s.name
    """
    with driver.session() as session:
        results = session.run(query, name=disease_name)
        return [record["s.name"] for record in results]

symptoms = query_symptoms("COVID-19")
print(f"Symptoms of COVID-19: {symptoms}")
```

5.3.2 RDFLib

- **Purpose**: Works with RDF data, including creating triples and querying with SPARQL.

- **Example**:

python

```
from rdflib.plugins.sparql import prepareQuery

# SPARQL query example
q = prepareQuery(
    "SELECT ?subject WHERE { ?subject <http://example.org/developed>
?object }"
)
for row in g.query(q):
    print(row.subject)
```

5.3.3 Transformers

- **Purpose**: Provides pre-trained transformer models for text generation and question answering.

- **Installation**:

bash

```
pip install transformers
```

- **Example**:

python

```
from transformers import pipeline

# Load a pre-trained model
generator = pipeline("text-generation", model="gpt-3.5")
```

```
# Generate text
result = generator("Explain the Theory of Relativity.", max_length=50)
print(result[0]["generated_text"])
```

5.3.4 NetworkX

- **Purpose**: Simplifies graph creation and manipulation in Python.

- **Example**:

python

```
import networkx as nx
import matplotlib.pyplot as plt

# Create a graph
G = nx.DiGraph()
G.add_edge("Albert Einstein", "Theory of Relativity",
relation="developed")
G.add_edge("Albert Einstein", "Germany", relation="born in")

# Visualize the graph
pos = nx.spring_layout(G)
nx.draw(G, pos, with_labels=True, node_color="skyblue",
node_size=3000)
plt.show()
```

5.3.5 Pandas

- **Purpose**: Handles tabular data that can complement knowledge graph workflows.

- **Example**: Importing CSV data into a Neo4j graph:

python

```
import pandas as pd
from neo4j import GraphDatabase

# Load CSV data
data = pd.read_csv("data.csv")

# Insert data into Neo4j
def load_data():
    query = """
    UNWIND $rows AS row
    CREATE (:Person {name: row.name, country: row.country})
    """
    with driver.session() as session:
        session.run(query, rows=data.to_dict("records"))

load_data()
```

Summary

- **Installing Required Tools**: Set up Python, Neo4j, and key libraries to establish a functional Graph RAG environment.

- **Knowledge Graph Platforms**: Use platforms like Neo4j, RDFLib, and Amazon Neptune for graph storage and querying.

- **Python Libraries**: Tools like networkx, transformers, and pandas enable seamless integration of LLMs with knowledge graphs.

5.4 Dataset Preparation and Integration

Preparing and integrating datasets is a crucial step in building a knowledge graph. Proper dataset preparation ensures the graph is accurate, well-structured, and useful for reasoning tasks.

5.4.1 Sources of Data for Knowledge Graphs

1. **Open Data Sources**:

   o **Wikidata**: A large, collaborative knowledge base.

   o **DBpedia**: Structured information extracted from Wikipedia.

   o **Kaggle Datasets**: A wide variety of domain-specific datasets.

2. **Domain-Specific Data**:

   o **Medical Data**: Clinical trials, PubMed articles, SNOMED CT.

   o **Financial Data**: SEC filings, market trends, transaction logs.

   o **Legal Data**: Case law, statutes, regulatory documents.

3. **Custom Datasets**:

   o Proprietary organizational data such as customer records, product catalogs, or internal research.

5.4.2 Data Cleaning

Raw datasets often contain inconsistencies or incomplete entries. Cleaning ensures that the data imported into the knowledge graph is high quality.

- **Deduplication**:

   o Merge identical records with minor differences.

   o Example: "Albert Einstein" and "Einstein, Albert."

- **Handling Missing Values**:

   o Use default values, infer relationships, or exclude incomplete records.

- **Normalization**:
  - Ensure consistency in naming conventions and formatting.
  - Example: Standardize dates to ISO 8601 (YYYY-MM-DD).
- **Code Example**: Cleaning a CSV dataset with Python:

python

```python
import pandas as pd

# Load dataset
data = pd.read_csv("data.csv")

# Drop duplicates
data = data.drop_duplicates()

# Fill missing values
data["birth_date"] = data["birth_date"].fillna("Unknown")

# Standardize case
data["name"] = data["name"].str.title()

# Save cleaned data
data.to_csv("cleaned_data.csv", index=False)
```

5.4.3 Data Transformation

To integrate data into a knowledge graph, it must be transformed into a format compatible with the graph database.

1. **CSV to Graph Nodes and Edges**:
   - Convert CSV rows into nodes and relationships.

- Example: A table of authors and their works can create Author and Book nodes with WROTE relationships.

2. **RDF Triples**:
   - Represent data as subject-predicate-object triples.
   - Example: (Albert Einstein, developed, Theory of Relativity).

3. **JSON for API Integration**:
   - Use JSON to import data into graph databases via APIs.

5.4.4 Data Loading into Graph Databases

- **Neo4j**:
  - Use the LOAD CSV command:

cypher

```
LOAD CSV WITH HEADERS FROM "file:///cleaned_data.csv" AS row
CREATE (:Person {name: row.name, birth_date: row.birth_date})
```

- **RDFLib**:
  - Import RDF triples:

python

```
from rdflib import Graph

g = Graph()
g.parse("data.rdf", format="xml")
print(f"Loaded {len(g)} triples")
```

5.5 Troubleshooting Installation Issues

Despite following installation guides, you may encounter issues. Below are common problems and their solutions:

5.5.1 Python Package Installation Issues

1. **Error: Package Not Found**:

   o **Cause**: Incorrect package name or version mismatch.

   o **Solution**:

bash

```
pip install <package-name>
pip install <package-name>==<specific-version>
```

2. **Error: Dependency Conflicts**:

   o **Cause**: Conflicting dependencies among installed libraries.

   o **Solution**:

      ▪ Use pip list to check installed versions.

      ▪ Create a fresh virtual environment.

5.5.2 Neo4j Connection Issues

1. **Error: Unable to Connect to Neo4j**:

   o **Cause**: Neo4j server not running or incorrect credentials.

   o **Solution**:

      ▪ Ensure the server is running:

bash

```
./bin/neo4j status
```

- Verify username and password.

2. **Error: File Import Fails**:

   o **Cause**: Incorrect file path or permissions.

   o **Solution**:

     - Place the file in the import folder of the Neo4j database directory.

     - Use the correct file path in queries:

cypher

```
LOAD CSV FROM "file:///data.csv" AS row
```

5.5.3 Graph Library Compatibility

1. **Error: Unsupported Graph Format**:

   o **Cause**: Mismatch between data format and graph library.

   o **Solution**:

     - Convert data into a compatible format, such as CSV, JSON, or RDF.

2. **Error: Library Version Issues**:

   o **Cause**: Outdated or incompatible library versions.

   o **Solution**:

bash

```
pip install --upgrade <library-name>
```

5.5.4 General Debugging Tips

- Check error logs for detailed messages.
- Ensure all dependencies are installed using:

bash

```
pip freeze > requirements.txt
pip install -r requirements.txt
```

- Consult documentation for library-specific troubleshooting.

5.6 Practice Problem: Setting Up a Graph Database

This exercise guides you through setting up a basic graph database in Neo4j and performing simple operations.

Problem Statement

1. Install Neo4j and start the database server.
2. Import a dataset of diseases and symptoms into the graph.
3. Query the graph to retrieve all symptoms of a specific disease.

Steps to Solve

1. **Install and Start Neo4j:**
   - Download Neo4j from neo4j.com.
   - Start the server:

bash

```
./bin/neo4j start
```

2. **Prepare the Dataset**:

- o Create a CSV file (disease_symptoms.csv):

csv

Disease,Symptom
COVID-19,Fever
COVID-19,Cough
Influenza,Fever
Influenza,Headache

3. **Load Data into Neo4j**:

- o Use the following Cypher query:

cypher

```
LOAD CSV WITH HEADERS FROM "file:///disease_symptoms.csv" AS
row
MERGE (d:Disease {name: row.Disease})
MERGE (s:Symptom {name: row.Symptom})
MERGE (d)-[:CAUSES]->(s)
```

4. **Query the Graph**:

- o Retrieve symptoms of a disease:

cypher

```
MATCH (d:Disease {name: "COVID-19"})-[:CAUSES]->(s:Symptom)
RETURN s.name AS symptom
```

Output:

plaintext

symptom

Fever

Cough

Code Example: Automating with Python

python

```
from neo4j import GraphDatabase

# Connect to Neo4j
driver = GraphDatabase.driver("bolt://localhost:7687", auth=("neo4j",
"password"))

# Load data into Neo4j
def load_data():
    query = """
    LOAD CSV WITH HEADERS FROM "file:///disease_symptoms.csv"
AS row
    MERGE (d:Disease {name: row.Disease})
    MERGE (s:Symptom {name: row.Symptom})
    MERGE (d)-[:CAUSES]->(s)
    """
    with driver.session() as session:
        session.run(query)

# Query the graph
def query_symptoms(disease_name):
    query = """
    MATCH (d:Disease {name: $name})-[:CAUSES]->(s:Symptom)
    RETURN s.name AS symptom
    """
```

```
with driver.session() as session:
    result = session.run(query, name=disease_name)
    return [record["symptom"] for record in result]

# Run the workflow
load_data()
symptoms = query_symptoms("COVID-19")
print(f"Symptoms of COVID-19: {symptoms}")
```
Output:

plaintext

Symptoms of COVID-19: ['Fever', 'Cough']

Summary

1. **Dataset Preparation and Integration**: Clean, transform, and load datasets into graph databases to ensure accurate and structured knowledge graphs.

2. **Troubleshooting Installation Issues**: Address common challenges with Python packages, Neo4j connections, and library compatibility.

3. **Practice Problem**: Step-by-step setup of a Neo4j graph database demonstrates practical implementation of knowledge graphs.

The next chapter will focus on designing and optimizing knowledge graphs for specific applications in Graph RAG workflows.

Chapter 6: Building a Knowledge Graph for LLMs

6.1 Designing a Knowledge Graph Schema

A well-designed schema is the backbone of any knowledge graph, defining how entities and relationships are structured. When building a knowledge graph for integration with LLMs, the schema must balance complexity and usability.

6.1.1 Key Components of a Schema

1. **Entities (Nodes)**:
   - Represent objects, concepts, or things in the graph.
   - **Examples**: "Albert Einstein," "Theory of Relativity," "Physics."

2. **Relationships (Edges)**:
   - Define how entities are connected.
   - **Examples**: "DEVELOPED," "BELONGS_TO," "LOCATED_IN."

3. **Attributes**:
   - Metadata for nodes and edges.
   - **Examples**:
     - Node Attribute: {name: "Einstein", born: 1879}
     - Edge Attribute: {confidence: 0.9}

4. **Constraints**:
   - Define rules for consistency and integrity.
   - **Examples**:

- A "Person" node must have a "name" attribute.

- A "DEVELOPED" relationship must connect "Person" and "Theory" nodes.

6.1.2 Steps to Design a Schema

1. **Identify Entities and Relationships**:
   - List the main entities and their connections.
   - Example for a medical knowledge graph:
     - Entities: Diseases, Symptoms, Treatments.
     - Relationships: "HAS_SYMPTOM," "TREATED_BY."

2. **Define Node and Edge Properties**:
   - Add attributes to enrich the graph.
   - Example:
     - Node: Disease {name: "COVID-19", type: "Viral"}
     - Edge: HAS_SYMPTOM {relevance: 0.95}

3. **Choose a Data Model**:
   - RDF model (triples: subject-predicate-object).
   - Property Graph model (nodes and edges with properties).

6.1.3 Schema Example: Academic Knowledge Graph

Entity Type	Attributes	Relationships
Person	name, birth_year, field	DEVELOPED → Theory

Entity Type	Attributes	Relationships
Theory	name, year_published	BELONGS_TO → Field
Field	name	
Institution	name, location	LOCATED_IN → Location
Location	name, country	

6.1.4 Cypher Example: Creating a Schema

cypher

```
// Create nodes
CREATE (einstein:Person {name: "Albert Einstein", birth_year: 1879,
field: "Physics"})
CREATE (relativity:Theory {name: "Theory of Relativity",
year_published: 1905})
CREATE (physics:Field {name: "Physics"})

// Create relationships
CREATE (einstein)-[:DEVELOPED]->(relativity)
CREATE (relativity)-[:BELONGS_TO]->(physics)
```

6.2 Data Sources for Populating Knowledge Graphs

Once the schema is designed, the next step is to gather data for populating the knowledge graph. The quality of the data directly impacts the graph's usability.

6.2.1 Types of Data Sources

1. **Open Data Repositories**:
   - **Examples**:
     - **Wikidata**: Structured data for entities and relationships.
     - **DBpedia**: RDF-based knowledge extracted from Wikipedia.

2. **Domain-Specific Databases**:
   - **Examples**:
     - Medical: PubMed, SNOMED CT.
     - Legal: Case law repositories.
     - Finance: SEC filings, stock market data.

3. **APIs**:
   - Fetch data programmatically for dynamic updates.
   - **Examples**:
     - Google Knowledge Graph API.
     - OpenWeatherMap API for location-based graphs.

4. **Custom Data**:
   - Proprietary data tailored to organizational needs.
   - **Examples**:
     - Customer relationship data.
     - Internal product catalogs.

6.2.2 Data Preparation Workflow

1. **Data Collection**:
   - Consolidate data from multiple sources.

2. **Data Cleaning**:

   o Handle missing, duplicate, or inconsistent data.

3. **Data Transformation**:

   o Convert raw data into graph-compatible formats (e.g., CSV, RDF).

4. **Data Validation**:

   o Ensure data complies with the graph schema.

6.2.3 Example: Academic Knowledge Graph Data

Person	Theory	Field	Institution
Albert Einstein	Theory of Relativity	Physics	ETH Zurich
Isaac Newton	Laws of Motion	Physics	University of Cambridge

6.2.4 Cypher Query: Loading Data

cypher

```
LOAD CSV WITH HEADERS FROM "file:///academic_data.csv" AS
row
MERGE (p:Person {name: row.Person})
MERGE (t:Theory {name: row.Theory})
MERGE (f:Field {name: row.Field})
MERGE (i:Institution {name: row.Institution})
MERGE (p)-[:DEVELOPED]->(t)
MERGE (t)-[:BELONGS_TO]->(f)
MERGE (p)-[:AFFILIATED_WITH]->(i)
```

6.3 Tools for Automating Knowledge Graph Construction

Manually constructing a knowledge graph is feasible for small datasets but impractical for large or dynamic systems. Automation tools streamline this process.

6.3.1 Graph Database Tools

1. **Neo4j**:

   o Provides Cypher for automated data import.

   o Supports integrations with Python for custom workflows.

2. **Amazon Neptune**:

   o Managed service with support for Gremlin and SPARQL.

6.3.2 Data Integration Tools

1. **Apache Nifi**:

   o Automates data flow between systems.

   o Ideal for combining data from APIs, files, and databases.

2. **ETL Tools (Extract, Transform, Load)**:

   o **Examples**:

      ▪ Talend.

      ▪ Pentaho.

   o Automatically process and transform raw data into graph-ready formats.

6.3.3 Python Libraries

1. **RDFlib**:

   o Automates RDF graph creation and SPARQL querying.

   o **Example**:

python

```
from rdflib import Graph
g = Graph()
g.add(("Albert_Einstein", "developed", "Theory_of_Relativity"))
```

2. **NetworkX**:

   o Automates creation and visualization of property graphs.

   o **Example**:

python

```
import networkx as nx
G = nx.DiGraph()
G.add_edge("Albert Einstein", "Theory of Relativity",
relation="developed")
```

6.3.4 Machine Learning-Based Tools

1. **DeepDive**:

   o Extracts structured information from unstructured data.

   o Ideal for populating graphs from text.

2. **Snorkel**:

   o Enables weak supervision to label large datasets.

Summary

1. **Designing a Knowledge Graph Schema**: A schema defines entities, relationships, and attributes, ensuring consistency and usability.

2. **Data Sources**: Use a combination of open repositories, APIs, and custom data for graph population.

3. **Automation Tools**: Platforms like Neo4j, RDFlib, and ETL tools simplify the construction and management of knowledge graphs.

6.4 Handling Data Inconsistencies and Noise

Data inconsistencies and noise are common challenges when building knowledge graphs. Addressing these issues ensures the graph's accuracy, reliability, and usability.

6.4.1 Common Data Issues

1. **Duplicate Entries**:

   o Same entity represented multiple times with slight variations.

   o **Example**: "Albert Einstein" vs. "Einstein, Albert."

2. **Conflicting Data**:

   o Discrepancies in data from multiple sources.

   o **Example**: Different birth dates for the same person.

3. **Incomplete Data**:

   o Missing attributes or relationships.

   o **Example**: A node for "COVID-19" without associated symptoms.

4. **Incorrect Data**:

    o   Erroneous entries.

    o   **Example**: A relationship stating "Albert Einstein is a country."

6.4.2 Techniques to Handle Data Inconsistencies

1. **Deduplication**:

    o   Identify and merge duplicate entities.

    o   **Approach**:

        ▪   Use unique identifiers (e.g., a UUID or standardized naming convention).

        ▪   Apply similarity measures (e.g., Levenshtein distance).

2. **Conflict Resolution**:

    o   Prioritize trusted sources when discrepancies arise.

    o   **Example**: Prefer data from verified APIs like Wikidata.

3. **Data Enrichment**:

    o   Fill missing information using additional sources or inferential techniques.

    o   **Example**: Infer the relationship "Einstein → DEVISED → Theory of Relativity" from context.

4. **Validation Rules**:

    o   Define constraints to ensure data integrity.

    o   **Example**: A "Person" node must have a "name" attribute.

6.4.3 Code Example: Handling Duplicate Entries

python

```python
import pandas as pd

# Sample dataset
data = pd.DataFrame({
    "Entity": ["Albert Einstein", "Einstein, Albert", "Isaac Newton",
"Newton, Isaac"],
    "Field": ["Physics", "Physics", "Mathematics", "Mathematics"]
})

# Deduplicate using similarity (e.g., name matching)
data["Entity"] = data["Entity"].str.lower().str.replace(",", "").str.strip()
deduplicated = data.drop_duplicates(subset="Entity")
print(deduplicated)
```

Output:

plaintext

```
       Entity       Field
0  albert einstein   Physics
2  isaac newton  Mathematics
```

6.5 Visualizing Knowledge Graphs

Visualization helps you explore and understand the structure of a knowledge graph by representing nodes, edges, and relationships visually.

6.5.1 Importance of Visualization

1. **Insights**: Highlights patterns and connections.

2. **Debugging**: Identifies anomalies and missing links.

3. **Explainability**: Provides clarity for non-technical stakeholders.

6.5.2 Popular Visualization Tools

1. **Neo4j Bloom**:

   o Built-in visualization tool for Neo4j.

   o Supports natural language-based graph exploration.

2. **Gephi**:

   o Open-source tool for graph visualization and manipulation.

   o Suitable for large graphs with clustering and filtering options.

3. **NetworkX with Matplotlib**:

   o Python-based solution for creating simple visualizations.

   o **Code Example**:

python

```python
import networkx as nx
import matplotlib.pyplot as plt

# Create a graph
G = nx.DiGraph()
G.add_edge("Albert Einstein", "Theory of Relativity",
relation="developed")
G.add_edge("Albert Einstein", "Physics", relation="studied")
G.add_edge("Theory of Relativity", "Physics", relation="belongs to")

# Draw the graph
pos = nx.spring_layout(G)
```

```
nx.draw(G, pos, with_labels=True, node_color="skyblue",
node_size=3000)
nx.draw_networkx_edge_labels(G, pos, edge_labels={
    ("Albert Einstein", "Theory of Relativity"): "developed",
    ("Albert Einstein", "Physics"): "studied",
    ("Theory of Relativity", "Physics"): "belongs to"
})
plt.show()
```

4. **Output**: A simple graph showing "Albert Einstein" connected to "Theory of Relativity" and "Physics."

6.5.3 Key Visualization Metrics

1. **Degree Centrality**:

   o Identifies nodes with the most connections.

   o **Example**: In a social network, "degree centrality" highlights the most influential individuals.

2. **Cluster Coefficient**:

   o Measures how closely nodes are connected within a group.

3. **Shortest Path**:

   o Identifies the shortest route between two nodes.

6.6 Code Example: Creating a Simple Knowledge Graph in Neo4j

This example demonstrates the complete workflow for creating and querying a knowledge graph in Neo4j.

6.6.1 Setting Up the Neo4j Environment

1. Install Neo4j.

2. Start the server:

bash

./bin/neo4j start

6.6.2 Populating the Knowledge Graph

-   Use the Cypher query language to create nodes and relationships.

cypher

```
// Create nodes
CREATE (einstein:Person {name: "Albert Einstein", birth_year: 1879})
CREATE (relativity:Theory {name: "Theory of Relativity", year: 1905})
CREATE (physics:Field {name: "Physics"})
CREATE (germany:Country {name: "Germany"})

// Create relationships
CREATE (einstein)-[:DEVELOPED]->(relativity)
CREATE (relativity)-[:BELONGS_TO]->(physics)
CREATE (einstein)-[:BORN_IN]->(germany)
```

6.6.3 Querying the Knowledge Graph

Retrieve data using Cypher queries.

1. **Query: Retrieve All Theories Developed by Einstein**:

cypher

```
MATCH (p:Person {name: "Albert Einstein"})-[:DEVELOPED]->(t:Theory)
RETURN t.name, t.year
```

Output:

plaintext

t.name   t.year

Theory of Relativity   1905

2. Query: Find Einstein's Field of Study:

cypher

```
MATCH (p:Person {name: "Albert Einstein"})-[:DEVELOPED]-
>(t:Theory)-[:BELONGS_TO]->(f:Field)
RETURN f.name
```

Output:

plaintext

f.name

Physics

3. Query: List All Entities Connected to Einstein:

cypher

```
MATCH (p:Person {name: "Albert Einstein"})--(n)
RETURN n.name
```

Output:

plaintext

n.name

Theory of Relativity

Germany

6.6.4 Integrating Neo4j with Python

Automate graph creation and queries using Python.

python

```python
from neo4j import GraphDatabase

# Connect to Neo4j
driver = GraphDatabase.driver("bolt://localhost:7687", auth=("neo4j",
"password"))

# Query function
def query_theories():
    query = """
    MATCH (p:Person {name: $name})-[:DEVELOPED]->(t:Theory)
    RETURN t.name AS theory, t.year AS year
    """
    with driver.session() as session:
        result = session.run(query, name="Albert Einstein")
        return [record for record in result]

# Fetch results
theories = query_theories()
for theory in theories:
    print(f"Theory: {theory['theory']}, Year: {theory['year']}")
```

Output:

plaintext

Summary

1. **Handling Data Inconsistencies**: Clean and validate data to maintain accuracy and consistency in the graph.

2. **Visualizing Knowledge Graphs**: Use tools like Neo4j Bloom, Gephi, or NetworkX to explore and analyze graph structures.

3. **Code Example**: A step-by-step Neo4j implementation highlights how to create and query a simple knowledge graph for practical use.

The next chapter will focus on integrating knowledge graphs with Retrieval-Augmented Generation (RAG) workflows for enhanced AI capabilities.

Chapter 7: Implementing Graph RAG

7.1 Setting Up the Graph Retrieval Module

The graph retrieval module is the backbone of a Graph RAG (Retrieval-Augmented Generation) system. It handles queries to the knowledge graph, retrieves relevant entities and relationships, and prepares data for integration with the Large Language Model (LLM).

7.1.1 Requirements

- **Graph Database**: A system like Neo4j, Amazon Neptune, or RDFLib for storing and querying graph data.

- **Graph Query Language**: Tools like Cypher, SPARQL, or Gremlin for efficient data retrieval.

- **APIs**: Enable integration between the graph database and LLM inputs.

7.1.2 Workflow for Graph Retrieval Module

1. **Input Query**:

   o   User input is parsed and converted into a structured query (e.g., Cypher or SPARQL).

2. **Query Execution**:

   o   Execute the query on the graph database to fetch relevant nodes and edges.

3. **Data Formatting**:

○ Convert retrieved data into a format compatible with the LLM.

7.1.3 Code Example: Setting Up Graph Retrieval Using Neo4j with Python:

python

```python
from neo4j import GraphDatabase

class GraphRetriever:
    def __init__(self, uri, user, password):
        self.driver = GraphDatabase.driver(uri, auth=(user, password))

    def close(self):
        self.driver.close()

    def retrieve_data(self, query, parameters=None):
        with self.driver.session() as session:
            result = session.run(query, parameters)
            return [record for record in result]

# Instantiate and connect to Neo4j
retriever = GraphRetriever("bolt://localhost:7687", "neo4j", "password")

# Sample query: Retrieve all theories developed by a specific person
query = """
MATCH (p:Person {name: $name})-[:DEVELOPED]->(t:Theory)
RETURN t.name AS theory, t.year AS year
"""
parameters = {"name": "Albert Einstein"}
data = retriever.retrieve_data(query, parameters)

# Display results
```

```
for record in data:
    print(f"Theory: {record['theory']}, Year: {record['year']}")

retriever.close()
```
Output:

plaintext

Theory: Theory of Relativity, Year: 1905

7.2 Implementing Graph Traversal Algorithms

Graph traversal is essential for exploring relationships between nodes, enabling multi-hop reasoning in Graph RAG systems.

7.2.1 Types of Graph Traversal

1. **Depth-First Search (DFS)**:

    o Explores as far as possible along a branch before backtracking.

    o **Use Case**: Finding all possible pathways between two entities.

2. **Breadth-First Search (BFS)**:

    o Explores all neighbors at the current depth level before moving deeper.

    o **Use Case**: Shortest path calculation.

3. **Shortest Path Algorithms**:

    o Finds the shortest path between two nodes.

- **Use Case**: Determining the quickest connection in a transportation graph.

7.2.2 Code Example: BFS for Graph Traversal

Using Python's NetworkX:

python

```
import networkx as nx

# Create a directed graph
G = nx.DiGraph()
G.add_edges_from([
    ("Albert Einstein", "Theory of Relativity"),
    ("Theory of Relativity", "Physics"),
    ("Albert Einstein", "Germany"),
    ("Physics", "Science")
])

# Perform BFS to find connections
bfs_edges = list(nx.bfs_edges(G, source="Albert Einstein"))
print("Breadth-First Search Edges:", bfs_edges)
```

Output:

plaintext

```
Breadth-First Search Edges: [('Albert Einstein', 'Theory of Relativity'), ('Albert Einstein', 'Germany'), ('Theory of Relativity', 'Physics')]
```

7.2.3 Cypher Query for Multi-Hop Traversal

Example: Find all nodes connected to "Albert Einstein" within 2 hops:

cypher

```
MATCH (p:Person {name: "Albert Einstein"})-[:DEVELOPED*..2]-(n)
RETURN DISTINCT n.name
```

Output:

plaintext

```
n.name

------------

Theory of Relativity

Physics
```

7.3 Integrating Graph Data with LLM Inputs

To leverage the retrieved graph data, it must be integrated with LLMs for generating enriched, contextual responses.

7.3.1 Workflow for Integration

1. **Retrieve Data**:
    - o Execute a graph query and collect nodes, edges, and attributes.
2. **Format Data**:
    - o Convert graph data into a textual prompt or structured input.
3. **LLM Interaction**:
    - o Pass the formatted data as context to the LLM.

7.3.2 Example: Formatting Graph Data for LLM

Retrieve and Format Data:

python

```
def format_graph_data(data):
    formatted = []
    for record in data:
        formatted.append(f"{record['theory']} (published in
{record['year']})")
    return "\n".join(formatted)

# Format the retrieved data
context = format_graph_data(data)
print("Context for LLM:")
print(context)
```

Output:

plaintext

```
Context for LLM:

Theory of Relativity (published in 1905)
```

7.3.3 Example: LLM Query with Graph Context

Using Hugging Face Transformers:

python

```
from transformers import pipeline

# Load a pre-trained model
```

```
generator = pipeline("text-generation", model="gpt-3.5")

# Generate a response using the graph context
query = "Explain the contributions of Albert Einstein based on the
following:"
prompt = f"{query}\n\n{context}"
response = generator(prompt, max_length=100)
print(response[0]["generated_text"])
```

Output:

plaintext

Albert Einstein contributed significantly to physics, particularly
through his Theory of Relativity, published in 1905. This
groundbreaking work revolutionized our understanding of space
and time.

7.3.4 Real-World Application

Use Case: Medical Knowledge Graph and LLM

- **Scenario**: A user queries, "What are the symptoms of
  COVID-19?"

- **Steps**:

    1. Query the knowledge graph for symptoms linked to
       COVID-19:

cypher

```
MATCH (d:Disease {name: "COVID-19"})-[:HAS_SYMPTOM]-
>(s:Symptom)
RETURN s.name
```

    2. Format the results as:

plaintext

COVID-19 is associated with the following symptoms:

- Fever

- Cough

- Fatigue

3. Pass this as context to the LLM for generating a detailed response:

python

```
prompt = "Explain COVID-19 symptoms based on the following
context:\n" + graph_context
```

Output:

plaintext

COVID-19 commonly presents symptoms such as fever, cough, and fatigue. These symptoms may vary in severity, and some individuals experience additional symptoms like loss of taste or smell.

Summary

1. **Setting Up the Graph Retrieval Module**: Establish robust graph querying capabilities using tools like Neo4j.

2. **Graph Traversal Algorithms**: Implement BFS, DFS, and shortest path algorithms for reasoning over graph data.

3. **Integration with LLMs**: Format retrieved graph data as input context to enable enriched and explainable AI outputs.

7.4 Multi-Hop Reasoning with Graph RAG

7.4.1 What is Multi-Hop Reasoning?

Multi-hop reasoning involves traversing multiple nodes and relationships in a knowledge graph to infer complex connections or retrieve in-depth answers. This capability makes Graph RAG systems powerful for tasks requiring advanced context and reasoning.

- **Example**: In a medical knowledge graph, finding treatments for a symptom linked through intermediate diseases:

    - **Path**: Symptom → Disease → Treatment.

7.4.2 Benefits of Multi-Hop Reasoning

1. **Contextual Depth**:

    - Provides richer, more meaningful answers by connecting distant but related nodes.

2. **Explainability**:

    - Traces the reasoning path, making AI decisions more transparent.

3. **Complex Query Handling**:

    - Solves multi-faceted queries, such as "What treatments exist for diseases causing fever?"

7.4.3 Example Use Case: Scientific Research

Query: "What are the practical applications of Einstein's theories?"

1. **Path**:

    - Albert Einstein → Theory of Relativity → Physics → Applications (e.g., GPS Technology).

2. **Graph Traversal**:

cypher

```
MATCH (person:Person {name: "Albert Einstein"})-[:DEVELOPED]-
>(theory:Theory)-[:APPLIED_IN]->(application:Application)
RETURN application.name
```

3. **Output:**

plaintext

application.name

GPS Technology

Time Dilation Research

7.4.4 Code Example: Multi-Hop Traversal with Python

python

```python
from neo4j import GraphDatabase

class MultiHopReasoner:
    def __init__(self, uri, user, password):
        self.driver = GraphDatabase.driver(uri, auth=(user, password))

    def close(self):
        self.driver.close()

    def multi_hop_query(self, start_node, end_node_label):
        query = f"""
        MATCH (start {{name: $start_node}})-[*]->(end:{end_node_label})
        RETURN end.name AS result
        """
        with self.driver.session() as session:
            results = session.run(query, start_node=start_node)
            return [record["result"] for record in results]
```

```
# Instantiate the reasoner
reasoner = MultiHopReasoner("bolt://localhost:7687", "neo4j",
"password")

# Multi-hop query
results = reasoner.multi_hop_query("Albert Einstein", "Application")
print("Applications of Einstein's theories:", results)

reasoner.close()
```
Output:

plaintext

Applications of Einstein's theories: ['GPS Technology', 'Time Dilation Research']

7.5 Tools and Platforms for Graph RAG Development

7.5.1 Graph Databases

1. **Neo4j**:

    o **Features**:

        ▪ Native graph storage and Cypher query language.

        ▪ Visualization tools like Neo4j Bloom.

    o **Use Case**: Suitable for large-scale multi-hop reasoning systems.

2. **Amazon Neptune**:

    o **Features**:

- Managed service supporting SPARQL and Gremlin.
        - Scales well with large datasets.
    - **Use Case**: Cloud-based graph systems for enterprise applications.

3. **ArangoDB**:

    - **Features**:

        - Multi-model database (graph, document, and key-value).

        - Supports AQL (Arango Query Language) for graph queries.

    - **Use Case**: Complex systems with hybrid data requirements.

7.5.2 Programming Libraries

1. **NetworkX**:

    - Python library for creating, analyzing, and visualizing graphs.

    - Ideal for small-scale or in-memory graph applications.

2. **RDFlib**:

    - Focused on RDF-based graphs and SPARQL queries.

    - Useful for semantic web and linked data projects.

3. **GraphQL**:

    - Query language for APIs that can be adapted for graph-based data.

7.5.3 Machine Learning Integration

1. **Deep Graph Library (DGL):**

    o Supports deep learning on graph structures.

    o Integrates with PyTorch and TensorFlow.

2. **PyTorch Geometric:**

    o Framework for graph neural networks (GNNs).

    o Enhances Graph RAG by learning from graph data.

7.5.4 Visualization Tools

1. **Gephi:**

    o Open-source graph visualization tool.

    o Provides clustering and centrality analysis.

2. **Neo4j Bloom:**

    o User-friendly visualization for Neo4j databases.

    o Supports natural language querying.

7.6 Optimizing Graph Traversal for Scalability

7.6.1 Challenges in Scalable Graph Traversal

1. **Large Graphs:**

    o Millions of nodes and edges can lead to performance bottlenecks.

2. **Complex Queries:**

    o Multi-hop queries require significant computational resources.

3. **Real-Time Constraints:**

- o Applications like chatbots demand low-latency responses.

7.6.2 Optimization Techniques

1. **Indexing**:

   - o Use graph database indexing to speed up node and edge lookups.

   - o **Example in Neo4j**:

cypher

```
CREATE INDEX ON :Person(name)
```

2. **Query Optimization**:

   - o Minimize unnecessary traversals by filtering at each step.

   - o **Example**: Add constraints to multi-hop queries:

cypher

```
MATCH (p:Person {name: "Albert Einstein"})-[:DEVELOPED]-
>(t:Theory)-[:APPLIED_IN]->(a:Application)
WHERE t.year > 1900
RETURN a.name
```

3. **Caching**:

   - o Store frequently accessed subgraphs in memory for quick retrieval.

4. **Parallel Processing**:

   - o Distribute graph traversal across multiple processors or servers.

   - o **Example**: Use Neo4j's multi-database architecture.

5. **Batch Processing**:

- o Precompute and store results for common queries.

7.6.3 Distributed Graph Systems

1. **Apache TinkerPop**:

    - o Framework for distributed graph processing.
    - o Includes Gremlin query language for traversal.

2. **TigerGraph**:

    - o Optimized for large-scale graph analytics.
    - o Supports parallel query execution.

7.6.4 Monitoring and Profiling

1. **Neo4j Query Profiling**:

    - o Use the PROFILE keyword to analyze query performance.
    - o **Example**:

cypher

```
PROFILE MATCH (p:Person {name: "Albert Einstein"})-
[:DEVELOPED]->(t:Theory)
RETURN t.name
```

    - o **Output**: Query execution plan and bottlenecks.

2. **Performance Metrics**:

    - o Monitor metrics like query execution time, memory usage, and traversal depth.

7.6.5 Example: Optimized Multi-Hop Query

cypher

```
// Use indexing and constraints for efficient multi-hop traversal
MATCH (p:Person {name: "Albert Einstein"})-[:DEVELOPED]-
>(t:Theory)-[:APPLIED_IN]->(a:Application)
WHERE t.year > 1900
RETURN DISTINCT a.name
```

Summary

1. **Multi-Hop Reasoning**: Enables complex queries by connecting distant nodes in the graph, improving the depth of insights.

2. **Tools and Platforms**: Neo4j, NetworkX, and DGL are key tools for Graph RAG development.

3. **Optimizing Graph Traversal**: Techniques like indexing, caching, and parallel processing improve scalability and performance.

7.7 Real-World Use Cases of Graph RAG Implementation

Graph RAG systems combine the contextual richness of knowledge graphs with the generative power of LLMs. Below are real-world use cases illustrating their potential across industries:

7.7.1 Healthcare

Use Case: Medical Diagnosis Support

- **Description**: A knowledge graph stores relationships between diseases, symptoms, and treatments. A Graph RAG system uses this graph to generate detailed diagnostic explanations and treatment plans.

- **Workflow**:

    1. Retrieve symptoms linked to a specific disease using multi-hop queries.

2. Pass retrieved data to an LLM to generate a comprehensive report.

- **Example**:
  - Query: "What are the symptoms and treatments for COVID-19?"
  - Graph Path: COVID-19 → HAS_SYMPTOM → Symptoms, COVID-19 → TREATED_BY → Treatments.

7.7.2 Legal Industry

Use Case: Case Law Research

- **Description**: A knowledge graph stores legal precedents, statutes, and case connections. The system answers complex legal questions by retrieving relevant cases and generating summaries.

- **Workflow**:
  1. Query legal connections (e.g., "precedent" or "mentioned in").
  2. Use the LLM to explain the connections in plain language.

- **Example**:
  - Query: "What precedents apply to contract disputes?"
  - Graph Path: Contract Disputes → MENTIONED_IN → Cases.

7.7.3 Academic Research

Use Case: Literature Review Generation

- **Description**: Graphs connect papers, authors, and topics. Researchers retrieve relevant citations and summaries with Graph RAG.

- **Workflow**:

   1. Find related works through CITED_BY and AUTHORED_BY relationships.

   2. LLM generates a summary of findings.

- **Example**:

   o Query: "What works cite Einstein's Theory of Relativity?"

   o Graph Path: Theory of Relativity → CITED_BY → Research Papers.

7.7.4 E-commerce

Use Case: Product Recommendations

- **Description**: Knowledge graphs link products, categories, and customer interactions. Graph RAG retrieves related products and generates personalized recommendations.

- **Workflow**:

   1. Traverse paths like BOUGHT_TOGETHER or VIEWED_AFTER.

   2. LLM personalizes recommendations based on user behavior.

- **Example**:

   o Query: "What should I buy with a smartphone?"

   o Graph Path: Smartphone → BOUGHT_TOGETHER → Accessories.

7.8 Code Example: Querying a Knowledge Graph with SPARQL

SPARQL is a powerful query language for RDF-based knowledge graphs. Below is an example of querying an academic knowledge graph.

7.8.1 Setting Up the RDF Graph

Use Python's rdflib to create and query an RDF knowledge graph.

Graph Construction:

python

```python
from rdflib import Graph, URIRef, Literal, Namespace

# Create a graph and namespace
g = Graph()
ex = Namespace("http://example.org/")

# Add nodes and edges
g.add((ex["Albert_Einstein"], ex["developed"],
ex["Theory_of_Relativity"]))
g.add((ex["Theory_of_Relativity"], ex["belongs_to"], ex["Physics"]))
g.add((ex["Albert_Einstein"], ex["born_in"], Literal("Germany")))

# Save the graph
g.serialize("academic_graph.rdf", format="xml")
print("Graph saved!")
```

7.8.2 Querying with SPARQL

Retrieve relationships from the graph using SPARQL.

Query Example:

python

```python
from rdflib.plugins.sparql import prepareQuery

# Define a SPARQL query
query = prepareQuery("""
    SELECT ?subject ?predicate ?object
    WHERE {
        ?subject ?predicate ?object
    }
""")

# Execute the query
results = g.query(query)

# Print results
for subj, pred, obj in results:
    print(f"{subj} -- {pred} --> {obj}")
```

Output:

plaintext

```
http://example.org/Albert_Einstein --
http://example.org/developed -->
http://example.org/Theory_of_Relativity

http://example.org/Theory_of_Relativity --
http://example.org/belongs_to --> http://example.org/Physics

http://example.org/Albert_Einstein -- http://example.org/born_in
--> Germany
```

7.9 Practice Problem: Building a Multi-Hop Retrieval Workflow

Problem Statement

You are tasked with designing a Graph RAG workflow for a medical knowledge graph. The graph connects diseases, symptoms, and treatments. The objective is to:

1. Query all symptoms of a disease.

2. Retrieve treatments for related diseases.

3. Pass the retrieved information to an LLM to generate a detailed response.

Steps to Solve

1. **Set Up the Knowledge Graph**:

   o Nodes: Disease, Symptom, Treatment.

   o Relationships: HAS_SYMPTOM, TREATED_BY.

Cypher Setup:

cypher

```
CREATE (covid:Disease {name: "COVID-19"})
CREATE (fever:Symptom {name: "Fever"})
CREATE (cough:Symptom {name: "Cough"})
CREATE (hydration:Treatment {name: "Hydration Therapy"})
CREATE (covid)-[:HAS_SYMPTOM]->(fever)
CREATE (covid)-[:HAS_SYMPTOM]->(cough)
CREATE (covid)-[:TREATED_BY]->(hydration)
```

2. **Write a Multi-Hop Query**:

o Find symptoms and treatments for diseases linked to COVID-19.

Query:

cypher

```cypher
MATCH (d:Disease {name: "COVID-19"})-[:HAS_SYMPTOM]->(s:Symptom)
WITH d, collect(s.name) AS symptoms
MATCH (d)-[:TREATED_BY]->(t:Treatment)
RETURN symptoms, collect(t.name) AS treatments
```

Output:

plaintext

symptoms: [Fever, Cough]

treatments: [Hydration Therapy]

---

3. **Format Results for LLM**: Pass the query results as context for an LLM.

Python Integration:

python

```python
from transformers import pipeline

# LLM pipeline
generator = pipeline("text-generation", model="gpt-3.5")

# Format graph data
context = """
Disease: COVID-19
Symptoms: Fever, Cough
```

Treatments: Hydration Therapy
"""

```
# Generate LLM response
prompt = f"Explain the details of COVID-19 based on the following
context:\n{context}"
response = generator(prompt, max_length=100)
print(response[0]["generated_text"])
```

Output:

plaintext

COVID-19 is a viral disease associated with symptoms such as fever and cough. Treatments include hydration therapy, which helps alleviate symptoms by maintaining fluid balance.

Summary

1. **Real-World Use Cases**: Graph RAG excels in healthcare, legal, academic, and e-commerce applications, providing enriched and explainable outputs.

2. **SPARQL Queries**: Efficiently retrieve data from RDF graphs for advanced reasoning.

3. **Practice Problem**: Building a multi-hop retrieval workflow integrates graph traversal with LLMs to address complex queries.

In the next chapter, we will explore evaluating and benchmarking Graph RAG systems to ensure their effectiveness and scalability in real-world applications.

Chapter 8: Knowledge Graph Integration in LLM Workflows

8.1 Querying Knowledge Graphs with SPARQL and Cypher

Querying knowledge graphs is a fundamental step in integrating them with LLMs. SPARQL and Cypher are two widely used query languages for RDF-based and property graph databases, respectively.

8.1.1 Querying with SPARQL

SPARQL (SPARQL Protocol and RDF Query Language) is used to query RDF-based graphs by matching patterns of triples (subject-predicate-object).

1. **Example Dataset**:

    o   Subject: Albert Einstein

    o   Predicate: developed

    o   Object: Theory of Relativity

SPARQL Query Example:

sparql

```
SELECT ?subject ?predicate ?object
WHERE {
  ?subject ?predicate ?object
}
```

Python Implementation:

python

```python
from rdflib import Graph

# Create an RDF graph
g = Graph()
g.parse("academic_graph.rdf", format="xml")

# Define SPARQL query
query = """
SELECT ?subject ?predicate ?object
WHERE {
  ?subject ?predicate ?object
}
"""

# Execute the query
results = g.query(query)

# Display results
for subj, pred, obj in results:
    print(f"{subj} -- {pred} --> {obj}")
```

Output:

plaintext

http://example.org/Albert_Einstein --
http://example.org/developed -->
http://example.org/Theory_of_Relativity

8.1.2 Querying with Cypher

Cypher is used with property graph databases like Neo4j to query nodes, relationships, and properties.

Example Dataset:

- Nodes: Albert Einstein, Theory of Relativity, Physics

- Relationships: DEVELOPED, BELONGS_TO

Cypher Query Example:

cypher

```cypher
MATCH (p:Person {name: "Albert Einstein"})-[:DEVELOPED]->(t:Theory)
RETURN t.name, t.year
```

Python Implementation:

python

```python
from neo4j import GraphDatabase

# Connect to Neo4j
driver = GraphDatabase.driver("bolt://localhost:7687", auth=("neo4j", "password"))

# Query function
def query_theory(person_name):
    query = """
    MATCH (p:Person {name: $name})-[:DEVELOPED]->(t:Theory)
    RETURN t.name AS theory, t.year AS year
    """
    with driver.session() as session:
        result = session.run(query, name=person_name)
        return [record for record in result]

# Fetch data
theories = query_theory("Albert Einstein")
for theory in theories:
    print(f"Theory: {theory['theory']}, Year: {theory['year']}")

driver.close()
```

Output:

plaintext

Theory: Theory of Relativity, Year: 1905

8.2 Combining Retrieved Graph Data with LLM Context Windows

LLMs operate within a limited context window, requiring retrieved graph data to be formatted and injected effectively. This step ensures that the retrieved information enriches the generative capabilities of the model.

8.2.1 Formatting Retrieved Data

1. **Structure**:

   o Present data as bullet points or natural language for clarity.

2. **Example**:

   o Retrieved Graph Data:

plaintext

Disease: COVID-19

Symptoms: Fever, Cough

Treatments: Hydration Therapy

8.2.2 Combining Data with Queries

- **Workflow**:

  1. Retrieve data from the knowledge graph.

  2. Format data into a structured prompt.

3. Concatenate user query and graph context.

Python Example:

python

```
from transformers import pipeline

# LLM pipeline
generator = pipeline("text-generation", model="gpt-3.5")

# Retrieved data
graph_context = """
Disease: COVID-19
Symptoms: Fever, Cough
Treatments: Hydration Therapy
"""

# User query
user_query = "Explain the symptoms and treatments of COVID-19."

# Combine query with graph context
prompt = f"{user_query}\n\nContext:\n{graph_context}"

# Generate response
response = generator(prompt, max_length=150)
print(response[0]["generated_text"])
```

Output:

plaintext

COVID-19 is associated with symptoms such as fever and cough. Treatments like hydration therapy are recommended to manage symptoms effectively.

8.3 Managing Context Length and Token Limits in LLMs

LLMs like GPT-3.5 and GPT-4 have a fixed token limit (e.g., 4096 tokens), which includes both the input and output. Properly managing context length is critical to ensure relevant information fits within the token budget.

8.3.1 Challenges

1. **Token Limitations**:
   - Excessive context can truncate the input or response.
2. **Prioritization**:
   - Not all retrieved data is equally relevant to the query.

8.3.2 Techniques to Manage Context

1. **Summarization**:
   - Use LLMs or graph-based summarization tools to condense retrieved data.
   - **Example**:

plaintext

Long Data: COVID-19 is caused by the SARS-CoV-2 virus. Symptoms include fever, cough, and fatigue.

Summarized Data: COVID-19 causes fever, cough, and fatigue.

2. **Selective Retrieval**:
   - Filter nodes and edges to include only query-relevant data.
   - **Cypher Example**:

cypher

```
MATCH (d:Disease {name: "COVID-19"})-[:HAS_SYMPTOM]-
>(s:Symptom)
WHERE s.relevance > 0.8
RETURN s.name
```

3. **Dynamic Context Windows**:

   o Dynamically adjust the amount of data included in the context window based on query complexity.

4. **Chunking**:

   o Break data into smaller, self-contained chunks and process them sequentially.

   o **Example**:

plaintext

Chunk 1: COVID-19 causes fever and cough.
Chunk 2: Treatments include hydration therapy.

8.3.3 Code Example: Managing Token Limits

python

```python
from transformers import pipeline

# Function to truncate context
def truncate_context(context, max_tokens):
    tokens = context.split()
    if len(tokens) > max_tokens:
        return " ".join(tokens[:max_tokens]) + "..."
    return context
```

```
# Graph context
graph_context = """
COVID-19 is caused by SARS-CoV-2. Symptoms include fever, cough,
and fatigue. Additional symptoms are loss of taste, headache, and
difficulty breathing. Hydration therapy and rest are commonly
recommended treatments. Severe cases may require hospitalization.
"""

# Truncate context to 100 tokens
truncated_context = truncate_context(graph_context, 100)
print("Truncated Context:", truncated_context)
```

Output:

plaintext

Truncated Context: COVID-19 is caused by SARS-CoV-2. Symptoms include fever, cough, and fatigue. Additional symptoms are loss of taste, headache, and difficulty breathing. Hydration therapy and rest are commonly recommended treatments...

Summary

1. **Querying Knowledge Graphs**:
   - SPARQL and Cypher provide robust methods for retrieving relevant data from knowledge graphs.

2. **Combining Graph Data with LLM Inputs**:
   - Format retrieved data and integrate it seamlessly with user queries to enrich LLM outputs.

3. **Managing Context Length**:
   - Use summarization, selective retrieval, and chunking to handle token limitations effectively.

8.4 Balancing Precision and Recall in Graph-Based Retrieval

Precision and recall are critical metrics in graph-based retrieval systems. They determine how effectively the system retrieves relevant nodes and relationships while minimizing irrelevant data.

8.4.1 Definitions

1. **Precision**:

   ○ The proportion of relevant nodes or edges retrieved out of the total retrieved.

   ○ **Formula**: $\text{Precision} = \dfrac{Relevant\ Retrieved\ Data}{Total\ Retrieved\ Data}$

2. **Recall**:

   ○ The proportion of relevant nodes or edges retrieved out of the total relevant data in the graph.

   ○ **Formula**: $\text{Recall} = \dfrac{Relevant\ Retrieved\ Data}{Total\ Relevant\ Data\ in\ Graph}$

3. **F1-Score**:

   ○ A harmonic mean of precision and recall: $F_1 = 2 \times \dfrac{Precision \times Recall}{Precision + Recall}$

8.4.2 Challenges

- **High Precision, Low Recall**:

  ○ May miss relevant data due to overly strict query constraints.

  ○ Example: A query for "diseases with symptoms fever AND cough" excludes diseases with only one of these symptoms.

- **High Recall, Low Precision**:

- o Retrieves excessive irrelevant data, making it harder to filter useful results.

- o Example: A query for "diseases with fever" retrieves all diseases linked to fever, including irrelevant cases.

8.4.3 Strategies for Balancing Precision and Recall

1. **Use Filters for Precision**:

   - o Apply constraints or thresholds.

   - o **Cypher Example**:

cypher

```
MATCH (d:Disease)-[:HAS_SYMPTOM]->(s:Symptom)
WHERE s.relevance > 0.8
RETURN d.name, s.name
```

2. **Expand Queries for Recall**:

   - o Allow broader criteria with optional matches.

   - o **SPARQL Example**:

sparql

```
SELECT ?disease ?symptom
WHERE {
  ?disease :hasSymptom ?symptom.
  OPTIONAL { ?disease :treatedBy ?treatment }
}
```

3. **Rank Results**:

   - o Use ranking algorithms to prioritize results by relevance.

   - o **Example**: Rank symptoms by relevance score.

4. **Iterative Refinement**:

- o Combine results from multiple queries with different scopes.

8.4.4 Code Example: Adjusting Precision and Recall

python

```python
def query_with_precision_or_recall(graph, high_precision=True):
    if high_precision:
        # Narrow query for high precision
        query = """
        MATCH (d:Disease)-[:HAS_SYMPTOM]->(s:Symptom)
        WHERE s.relevance > 0.9
        RETURN d.name, s.name
        """
    else:
        # Broad query for high recall
        query = """
        MATCH (d:Disease)-[:HAS_SYMPTOM]->(s:Symptom)
        RETURN d.name, s.name
        """

    results = graph.run(query)
    return results

# Example usage
high_precision_results = query_with_precision_or_recall(graph,
high_precision=True)
high_recall_results = query_with_precision_or_recall(graph,
high_precision=False)
```

8.5 Enhancing Generation with Contextual Knowledge

Integrating contextual knowledge from knowledge graphs into LLMs significantly improves the quality and relevance of generated responses.

8.5.1 Importance of Contextual Knowledge

1. **Informed Responses**:

   o Graph data provides structured context for answering domain-specific questions.

   o Example: A query about a disease retrieves its symptoms and treatments from the graph.

2. **Explainability**:

   o LLMs can generate responses with references to graph data, enhancing trust.

8.5.2 Workflow for Contextual Integration

1. **Retrieve Relevant Data**:

   o Use graph queries to extract specific knowledge.

2. **Format for LLM Input**:

   o Structure the retrieved data into readable prompts.

3. **Generate Responses**:

   o Use an LLM to process the prompt and provide an enriched answer.

8.5.3 Example: Enhancing Responses

Graph Data:

- Disease: COVID-19
- Symptoms: Fever, Cough
- Treatments: Hydration Therapy

Prompt:

plaintext

What is COVID-19?

Context:

- COVID-19 is a viral disease.

- Symptoms include fever and cough.

- Treatments include hydration therapy.

Python Code:

python

```python
from transformers import pipeline

# Initialize LLM
generator = pipeline("text-generation", model="gpt-3.5")

# Combine user query and graph context
query = "What is COVID-19?"
graph_context = """
- COVID-19 is a viral disease.
- Symptoms include fever and cough.
- Treatments include hydration therapy.
"""
prompt = f"{query}\n\nContext:\n{graph_context}"

# Generate response
response = generator(prompt, max_length=150)
```

```
print(response[0]["generated_text"])
```

Output:

plaintext

COVID-19 is a viral disease characterized by symptoms such as fever and cough. Treatments like hydration therapy are recommended for managing symptoms.

8.6 Case Study: Integrating Knowledge Graphs in Conversational AI

8.6.1 Scenario

Objective: Enhance a healthcare chatbot using a knowledge graph integrated with an LLM to provide detailed and accurate responses about diseases.

8.6.2 Workflow

1. **Knowledge Graph Setup**:

   o Nodes: Diseases, Symptoms, Treatments.

   o Relationships: HAS_SYMPTOM, TREATED_BY.

2. **Graph Query**:

   o Retrieve symptoms and treatments for a queried disease.

   o **Cypher Example**:

cypher

```
MATCH (d:Disease {name: "COVID-19"})-[:HAS_SYMPTOM]-
>(s:Symptom)
```

RETURN s.name AS symptoms

3. **Format for Chatbot**:

   o Structure retrieved data into a user-friendly format.

   o Example:

plaintext

COVID-19 Symptoms: Fever, Cough
Recommended Treatment: Hydration Therapy

4. **LLM Integration**:

   o Use the graph data to generate conversational responses.

8.6.3 Python Implementation

python

```python
from neo4j import GraphDatabase
from transformers import pipeline

# Initialize Neo4j connection and LLM
driver = GraphDatabase.driver("bolt://localhost:7687", auth=("neo4j",
"password"))
generator = pipeline("text-generation", model="gpt-3.5")

def get_graph_data(disease_name):
    query = """
    MATCH (d:Disease {name: $name})-[:HAS_SYMPTOM]-
>(s:Symptom)
    RETURN collect(s.name) AS symptoms
    """
    with driver.session() as session:
        result = session.run(query, name=disease_name).single()
```

```python
        return result["symptoms"]

def generate_response(disease_name):
    symptoms = get_graph_data(disease_name)
    graph_context = f"""
    Disease: {disease_name}
    Symptoms: {', '.join(symptoms)}
    """
    prompt = f"Explain details about
{disease_name}.\n\nContext:\n{graph_context}"
    response = generator(prompt, max_length=150)
    return response[0]["generated_text"]

# Example usage
response = generate_response("COVID-19")
print(response)
```

Output:

plaintext

COVID-19 is a disease characterized by symptoms such as fever and cough. Effective management includes hydration therapy and supportive care.

8.6.4 Benefits of Knowledge Graph Integration

1. **Accuracy**:

   o Graphs ensure retrieval of verified and structured information.

2. **Explainability**:

   o Chatbots can trace responses back to graph data.

3. **Scalability**:

o Graphs handle dynamic updates, ensuring the chatbot remains current.

Summary

1. **Balancing Precision and Recall**: Techniques like filtering and ranking ensure relevant data retrieval while avoiding overloading the system.

2. **Enhancing Generation**: Contextual knowledge from graphs improves response quality and relevance.

3. **Case Study**: Demonstrates the effectiveness of integrating knowledge graphs with conversational AI systems for real-world applications.

Chapter 9: Advanced Topics in Graph RAG

9.1 Handling Large-Scale Graphs Efficiently

As knowledge graphs grow in size, managing and querying millions of nodes and edges becomes challenging. Efficient handling of large-scale graphs is essential for real-time applications and scalable systems.

9.1.1 Challenges with Large-Scale Graphs

1. **High Storage Requirements**:

   o Large graphs demand significant disk and memory resources.

   o Example: Social networks or biomedical knowledge graphs.

2. **Slow Query Performance**:

   o Multi-hop queries can lead to long execution times.

   o Example: Finding all nodes within a 3-hop neighborhood.

3. **Concurrency Issues**:

   o Simultaneous queries from multiple users can cause bottlenecks.

9.1.2 Optimization Techniques

1. **Indexing**:

   o Create indexes on frequently queried properties to speed up lookups.

- o **Neo4j Example**:

cypher

2. **Partitioning**:
   - o Divide the graph into smaller subgraphs based on logical groupings (e.g., geography, topic).
   - o Use distributed systems like Amazon Neptune or Apache Giraph.

3. **Caching**:
   - o Store frequently accessed subgraphs or query results in memory.
   - o Example: Cache relationships of high-degree nodes like "Albert Einstein."

4. **Parallel Query Execution**:
   - o Leverage distributed computing to execute queries in parallel.
   - o **Example**: Use Neo4j's Enterprise Edition for cluster-based queries.

5. **Batch Processing**:
   - o Precompute and store results for common queries.
   - o Example: Precompute shortest paths between key nodes.

9.1.3 Distributed Graph Databases

1. **Amazon Neptune**:
   - o Fully managed graph database with built-in scalability.

o Supports SPARQL and Gremlin.

2. **TigerGraph**:

o Optimized for distributed storage and analytics.

o Suitable for real-time applications.

3. **JanusGraph**:

o Open-source graph database that scales with backend support like Cassandra or HBase.

9.1.4 Example: Optimizing Large Graph Queries

Scenario: Find all diseases related to COVID-19 within 3 hops.

Cypher Query:

cypher

```
MATCH (d:Disease {name: "COVID-19"})-[:RELATED*1..3]-
>(related:Disease)
RETURN DISTINCT related.name
```

Optimizations:

- Use an index on the Disease label.

- Precompute a 3-hop neighborhood for high-traffic nodes.

9.2 Dynamic Knowledge Graphs: Updates and Maintenance

Dynamic knowledge graphs adapt to evolving datasets, ensuring they remain accurate and relevant.

9.2.1 Characteristics of Dynamic Knowledge Graphs

1. **Real-Time Updates**:

o   Add or modify nodes and relationships as new data becomes available.

2. **Version Control**:

o   Maintain a history of changes for auditing and rollback.

3. **Consistency**:

o   Ensure updates do not introduce inconsistencies.

9.2.2 Challenges

1. **Concurrency**:

o   Multiple users or systems updating the graph simultaneously.

2. **Data Integrity**:

o   Avoid cycles or orphan nodes caused by incomplete updates.

9.2.3 Best Practices for Updates

1. **Transactional Updates**:

o   Use ACID-compliant databases to ensure atomicity.

o   **Example in Neo4j**:

cypher

```
BEGIN TRANSACTION
CREATE (:Symptom {name: "Fever"})
COMMIT
```

2. **Batch Updates**:

- o Process updates in bulk for efficiency.

- o **Example**: Load a CSV file containing new relationships:

cypher

```
LOAD CSV WITH HEADERS FROM "file:///updates.csv" AS row
MATCH (d:Disease {name: row.Disease})
MERGE (s:Symptom {name: row.Symptom})
MERGE (d)-[:HAS_SYMPTOM]->(s)
```

3. **Validation Rules**:

- o Implement rules to validate updates.

- o **Example**: Reject relationships with invalid node types.

9.2.4 Monitoring and Maintenance

1. **Monitoring Tools**:

- o Use tools like Prometheus or Grafana for real-time monitoring.

- o Track metrics such as query latency and update frequency.

2. **Maintenance Tasks**:

- o Periodically clean unused nodes and edges.

- o Backup the graph database regularly.

9.3 Graph Neural Networks for Advanced Reasoning

Graph Neural Networks (GNNs) extend traditional graph analytics by leveraging machine learning to infer patterns and predict relationships.

9.3.1 Overview of GNNs

1. **Purpose**:

   - Use graph structure and node features to predict properties or relationships.

   - Example: Predicting the likelihood of a new edge in the graph.

2. **Key Components**:

   - **Node Embeddings**: Represent nodes as dense vectors.

   - **Message Passing**: Aggregate information from neighbors.

   - **Graph Convolution**: Apply convolution operations to graph data.

9.3.2 Applications

1. **Link Prediction**:

   - Predict missing edges in incomplete graphs.

   - Example: Suggesting relationships in social networks.

2. **Node Classification**:

   - Predict the label of a node based on its features and neighbors.

   - Example: Classifying diseases based on symptoms.

3. **Graph Classification**:

   - Predict properties of an entire graph.

   - Example: Classifying molecular graphs in drug discovery.

9.3.3 Tools for GNN Development

1. **Deep Graph Library (DGL)**:

   o Supports GNNs with PyTorch and TensorFlow.

   o Example: Node classification on citation networks.

2. **PyTorch Geometric**:

   o Lightweight library for building GNNs.

   o Includes pre-built layers like GCNConv and GraphSAGE.

3. **Graph Nets**:

   o TensorFlow-based library for graph learning tasks.

9.3.4 Example: Node Classification with GCN

python

```python
import torch
import torch.nn.functional as F
from torch_geometric.nn import GCNConv
from torch_geometric.datasets import Planetoid

# Load a dataset
dataset = Planetoid(root="/tmp/Cora", name="Cora")

# Define the GCN model
class GCN(torch.nn.Module):
    def __init__(self):
        super(GCN, self).__init__()
        self.conv1 = GCNConv(dataset.num_node_features, 16)
        self.conv2 = GCNConv(16, dataset.num_classes)

    def forward(self, data):
```

```python
        x, edge_index = data.x, data.edge_index
        x = F.relu(self.conv1(x, edge_index))
        x = F.dropout(x, training=self.training)
        x = self.conv2(x, edge_index)
        return F.log_softmax(x, dim=1)

# Train the model
data = dataset[0]
model = GCN()
optimizer = torch.optim.Adam(model.parameters(), lr=0.01)

for epoch in range(200):
    model.train()
    optimizer.zero_grad()
    out = model(data)
    loss = F.nll_loss(out[data.train_mask], data.y[data.train_mask])
    loss.backward()
    optimizer.step()

# Evaluate
model.eval()
_, pred = model(data).max(dim=1)
accuracy = (pred[data.test_mask] == data.y[data.test_mask]).sum() /
data.test_mask.sum()
print(f"Accuracy: {accuracy:.2f}")
```

Output:

plaintext

Accuracy: 0.81

Summary

1. **Handling Large-Scale Graphs**:

- Use techniques like indexing, partitioning, and caching to optimize performance.

2. **Dynamic Knowledge Graphs**:

   - Ensure data integrity and support real-time updates with ACID-compliant operations.

3. **Graph Neural Networks**:

   - Leverage GNNs for advanced reasoning tasks like link prediction and node classification.

9.4 Incorporating Temporal and Spatial Knowledge

9.4.1 The Importance of Temporal and Spatial Knowledge

1. **Temporal Knowledge**:

   - Deals with time-sensitive relationships and events in the graph.

   - Example: A drug approval date or the timeline of scientific discoveries.

2. **Spatial Knowledge**:

   - Captures geographical or positional data.

   - Example: The location of diseases or the geographical distribution of resources.

Incorporating temporal and spatial dimensions into a Graph RAG system enhances its reasoning capabilities and contextual accuracy.

9.4.2 Modeling Temporal and Spatial Knowledge

1. **Temporal Graphs**:

   - Nodes and edges include timestamps to represent temporal validity.

- Example:
    - Node: COVID-19 Outbreak {start_date: "2019-12-01", end_date: "2022-12-01"}
    - Edge: RELATED_TO {timestamp: "2020-03-11"}.

2. **Spatial Graphs**:
    - Nodes and edges have location attributes such as latitude and longitude.
    - **Example**:
        - Node: Hospital {name: "City Hospital", location: [40.7128, -74.0060]}.
        - Edge: SERVES_AREA {region: "New York"}.

9.4.3 Querying Temporal and Spatial Graphs

1. **Cypher Query for Temporal Data**:
    - Retrieve events within a specific timeframe.

cypher

```
MATCH (e:Event)
WHERE e.start_date >= "2020-01-01" AND e.end_date <= "2020-12-31"
RETURN e.name
```

2. **Cypher Query for Spatial Data**:
    - Find nodes within a geographical area.

cypher

```
MATCH (h:Hospital)
WHERE h.location.latitude >= 40 AND h.location.latitude <= 41
RETURN h.name
```

3. **SPARQL Query for Temporal Data:**

   o Filter events based on timestamps.

sparql

```
SELECT ?event
WHERE {
  ?event :start_date ?date .
  FILTER (?date >= "2020-01-01"^^xsd:date && ?date <= "2020-12-
31"^^xsd:date)
}
```

9.4.4 Code Example: Temporal Query in Python

python

```python
from neo4j import GraphDatabase

class TemporalGraphQuery:
    def __init__(self, uri, user, password):
        self.driver = GraphDatabase.driver(uri, auth=(user, password))

    def close(self):
        self.driver.close()

    def query_temporal_events(self, start_date, end_date):
        query = """
        MATCH (e:Event)
        WHERE e.start_date >= $start_date AND e.end_date <= $end_date
        RETURN e.name AS event, e.start_date AS start, e.end_date AS end
        """
        with self.driver.session() as session:
            results = session.run(query, start_date=start_date,
end_date=end_date)
            return [record for record in results]
```

```
# Usage
query_tool = TemporalGraphQuery("bolt://localhost:7687", "neo4j",
"password")
events = query_tool.query_temporal_events("2020-01-01", "2020-12-31")
for event in events:
    print(f"Event: {event['event']}, Start: {event['start']}, End:
{event['end']}")
query_tool.close()
```

Output:

plaintext

Event: COVID-19 Outbreak, Start: 2020-01-01, End: 2020-12-31

9.5 Cross-Domain Applications of Graph RAG

Graph RAG systems can be applied across diverse domains, leveraging their ability to integrate structured knowledge graphs with generative AI.

9.5.1 Healthcare

- **Use Case**: Personalized treatment recommendations.
- **Workflow**:
    1. Query the graph for symptoms and treatments.
    2. Use LLMs to generate a patient-specific treatment plan.

9.5.2 Finance

- **Use Case**: Fraud detection in transactions.
- **Workflow**:
    1. Traverse transaction networks to detect anomalies.
    2. LLMs explain anomalies in plain language.

9.5.3 Education

- **Use Case**: Dynamic curriculum generation.
- **Workflow**:
    1. Link topics and prerequisites in an educational graph.
    2. Generate customized learning paths.

9.5.4 Supply Chain

- **Use Case**: Real-time logistics tracking.
- **Workflow**:
    1. Graph tracks inventory and transit.
    2. LLMs summarize bottlenecks and suggest optimizations.

9.6 Code Example: Scaling Graph Retrieval with Parallel Queries

Large-scale graphs require parallel processing to ensure fast and efficient retrieval.

9.6.1 Why Parallel Queries?

- **Problem**: Single-threaded queries may be slow for large graphs.

- **Solution**: Divide queries into smaller parts and execute them concurrently.

9.6.2 Implementation

Use Python's concurrent.futures for parallelizing graph queries.

Example Code:

python

```
from concurrent.futures import ThreadPoolExecutor
from neo4j import GraphDatabase

class ParallelGraphQuery:
    def __init__(self, uri, user, password):
        self.driver = GraphDatabase.driver(uri, auth=(user, password))

    def close(self):
        self.driver.close()

    def query(self, disease_name):
        query = """
        MATCH (d:Disease {name: $name})-[:HAS_SYMPTOM]-
>(s:Symptom)
        RETURN s.name AS symptom
        """
        with self.driver.session() as session:
            results = session.run(query, name=disease_name)
            return [record["symptom"] for record in results]

# Parallel processing
def fetch_symptoms(disease_name):
```

```
query_tool = ParallelGraphQuery("bolt://localhost:7687", "neo4j",
"password")
    symptoms = query_tool.query(disease_name)
    query_tool.close()
    return {disease_name: symptoms}

# Diseases to query
diseases = ["COVID-19", "Influenza", "Diabetes"]

# Execute queries in parallel
with ThreadPoolExecutor() as executor:
    results = list(executor.map(fetch_symptoms, diseases))

# Display results
for result in results:
    print(result)
```

Output:

plaintext

{'COVID-19': ['Fever', 'Cough']}

{'Influenza': ['Fever', 'Fatigue']}

{'Diabetes': ['Thirst', 'Blurred Vision']}

Summary

1. **Incorporating Temporal and Spatial Knowledge**:
   - Adds depth to graph data by modeling time-sensitive and geographical relationships.

2. **Cross-Domain Applications**:

    o   Graph RAG systems are versatile, spanning healthcare, finance, education, and more.

3. **Scaling Graph Retrieval**:

    o   Parallel queries significantly enhance retrieval performance for large-scale graphs.

Chapter 10: Applications of Graph RAG with LLMs

10.1 Personalized Recommendations

Graph RAG systems are transformative for building personalized recommendation engines by combining structured graph data with LLMs' generative abilities.

10.1.1 Algorithms and Graph Structures for Recommendations

Graph Structures for Recommendations:

1. **Nodes**:

   - Represent entities such as users, products, or preferences.

   - Example: User, Product, Category.

2. **Edges**:

   - Capture relationships like PURCHASED, VIEWED, LIKED, or SIMILAR_TO.

   - Example:

     - User1 → PURCHASED → ProductA

     - ProductA → SIMILAR_TO → ProductB

Key Algorithms:

1. **Collaborative Filtering**:

   - Leverages relationships between users and items to recommend products.

- **Graph Path**: User → PURCHASED → Product → PURCHASED_BY → Other Users.

2. **Content-Based Filtering**:

    o Uses node attributes to recommend similar items.

    o **Example**:

        ▪ Node Attribute: Product {category: "Electronics", brand: "Apple"}.

        ▪ Query: Find products in the same category and brand.

3. **Hybrid Models**:

    o Combine collaborative and content-based filtering.

    o Use edge weights to prioritize certain relationships.

Example Graph:

Node	Attributes	Edges
User1	{age: 30, location: US}	PURCHASED → ProductA
ProductA	{category: Electronics}	SIMILAR_TO → ProductB

10.1.2 Real-World Examples in E-Commerce

Use Case: Product Recommendations

1. **Workflow**:

    o Graph Query: Retrieve SIMILAR_TO and PURCHASED_BY relationships.

    o LLM Task: Generate a natural language explanation for recommendations.

2. **Example Query**:

cypher

```
MATCH (p:Product)-[:SIMILAR_TO]->(rec:Product)
WHERE p.name = "Smartphone"
RETURN rec.name
```

3. **Python Integration**:

python

```python
from transformers import pipeline

# Retrieved data
recommendations = ["Smartphone Case", "Wireless Charger"]

# LLM for explanation
generator = pipeline("text-generation", model="gpt-3.5")
prompt = f"Based on your interest in Smartphones, we recommend:\n-
{recommendations[0]}\n- {recommendations[1]}"
response = generator(prompt, max_length=150)
print(response[0]["generated_text"])
```

Output:

plaintext

Based on your interest in Smartphones, we recommend:

- Smartphone Case: To protect your phone.

- Wireless Charger: For convenient charging.

10.2 Healthcare

Graph RAG systems have immense potential in healthcare, improving diagnostics, treatment recommendations, and medical research.

10.2.1 Using Graph RAG for Symptom Diagnosis

1. **Graph Structure**:

   o Nodes: Disease, Symptom, Treatment.

   o Edges: HAS_SYMPTOM, TREATED_BY.

2. **Example Graph Query**:

cypher

```cypher
MATCH (d:Disease)-[:HAS_SYMPTOM]->(s:Symptom)
WHERE s.name IN ["Fever", "Cough"]
RETURN d.name, s.name
```

3. **Python Integration**:

python

```python
diseases = [{"name": "COVID-19", "symptoms": ["Fever", "Cough"]}]
prompt = f"Given the symptoms Fever and Cough, possible diseases are {diseases[0]['name']}."
response = generator(prompt, max_length=150)
print(response[0]["generated_text"])
```

Output:

plaintext

Given the symptoms Fever and Cough, possible diseases are COVID-19. It is recommended to consult a healthcare professional.

10.2.2 Medical Ontologies and Data Integration

Medical Ontologies:

1. **SNOMED CT**:
   - Standardized terminology for diseases and treatments.
   - Example: COVID-19 → Respiratory Disease.
2. **ICD-10**:
   - Classification of diseases.
   - Example: J12.82 → Pneumonia due to COVID-19.

Data Integration:

- Combine ontologies with real-world patient data.
- Example: Linking electronic health records (EHRs) to graph nodes.

10.3 Legal Research and Document Summarization

Graph RAG can transform legal workflows by simplifying research and automating document summaries.

10.3.1 Using Graphs for Legal Research

1. **Graph Structure**:
   - Nodes: Case, Statute, Legal Precedent.
   - Edges: MENTIONS, CITED_IN.
2. **Example Graph Query**:

cypher

```
MATCH (c:Case)-[:CITED_IN]->(p:Precedent)
WHERE c.name = "Brown v. Board of Education"
```

```
RETURN p.name
```

3. **LLM Integration**:

- o Graph Query: Retrieve cited cases.

- o LLM Task: Summarize retrieved cases.

10.3.2 Summarizing Legal Documents

1. **Workflow**:

- o Graph Query: Fetch related documents.

- o LLM Task: Generate summaries.

2. **Example Prompt**:

plaintext

Case: Brown v. Board of Education.

Cited Precedents:

- Plessy v. Ferguson: Segregation case in 1896.

Summary:

3. **Python Example**:

python

```python
cited_cases = ["Plessy v. Ferguson"]
prompt = f"Case: Brown v. Board of Education.\nCited Precedents:\n-
{cited_cases[0]}: Segregation case in 1896.\nSummary:"
response = generator(prompt, max_length=150)
print(response[0]["generated_text"])
```

Output:

plaintext

Case: Brown v. Board of Education challenged racial segregation in schools and overturned the precedent set by Plessy v. Ferguson.

10.3.3 Example Graph for Legal Research

Node	Attributes	Edges
Brown v. Board	{type: Case, year: 1954}	CITED_IN → Plessy
Plessy v. Ferguson	{type: Precedent, year: 1896}	

Summary

1. **Personalized Recommendations**:

   o Graph RAG combines graph-based relationships and LLMs to create meaningful recommendations.

2. **Healthcare**:

   o Use knowledge graphs for symptom diagnosis and integrating medical ontologies.

3. **Legal Research**:

   o Simplify complex legal queries and automate summarization of related cases and documents.

10.4 Scientific Discovery and Literature Mining

10.4.1 Multi-Hop Reasoning for Hypothesis Generation

Overview: Multi-hop reasoning enables the connection of disparate nodes in a knowledge graph, uncovering hidden relationships that can generate new hypotheses in scientific research.

Graph Structure:

1. **Nodes**:

   o   Entities such as Chemical, Gene, Disease, Publication.

   o   Example: Aspirin, Pain Relief, Article123.

2. **Edges**:

   o   Represent relationships like MENTIONS, ASSOCIATED_WITH, or CAUSAL_LINK.

   o   Example:

      ▪   Chemical → ASSOCIATED_WITH → Disease.

Use Case: Drug Discovery:

- **Workflow**:

   1. Use graph queries to identify unexplored connections between chemicals and diseases.

   2. Apply LLMs to interpret results and suggest hypotheses.

- **Example Query**:

cypher

```
MATCH (c:Chemical)-[:ASSOCIATED_WITH]->(d:Disease)
WHERE c.name = "Aspirin"
RETURN d.name
```

Python Example:

python

```python
from transformers import pipeline

# Mock data from graph
results = ["Pain Relief", "Inflammation"]

# Generate hypotheses with LLM
generator = pipeline("text-generation", model="gpt-3.5")
prompt = f"The chemical Aspirin is associated with:\n- {results[0]}\n-
{results[1]}.\nWhat potential hypotheses can be derived?"
response = generator(prompt, max_length=150)
print(response[0]["generated_text"])
```

Output:

plaintext

Aspirin is linked to pain relief and inflammation reduction. A
potential hypothesis could involve its application in treating
inflammatory diseases like arthritis.

10.5 Conversational AI and Context-Aware Chatbots

10.5.1 Leveraging Graph RAG for Long-Form Conversations

Overview: Graph RAG enhances chatbots by providing context-aware, detailed, and accurate responses through graph integration.

Workflow:

1. **Graph Query**:
   o Retrieve relevant data (e.g., user preferences, FAQs).

2. **LLM Generation**:
   o Use the retrieved data to generate responses.

3. **Multi-Turn Conversations**:
   o Maintain context across turns using the graph.

Example: FAQ Bot for Healthcare:

- **Graph Data**:
   o Nodes: Symptom, Treatment.
   o Edges: HAS_SYMPTOM, TREATED_BY.

- **Python Implementation**:

python

```
from transformers import pipeline

# Graph data for context
context = """
Symptom: Fever
Possible Diseases: COVID-19, Influenza
Recommended Treatments: Rest, Hydration
"""

# User query
query = "How do I treat a fever?"
```

```
# Combine query with context
prompt = f"{query}\n\nContext:\n{context}"
response = pipeline("text-generation", model="gpt-3.5")(prompt,
max_length=150)

# Display response
print(response[0]["generated_text"])
```

Output:

plaintext

To treat a fever, consider rest and hydration. If symptoms persist,
consult a healthcare professional for further guidance.

10.6 Educational Technology

10.6.1 Personalized Learning Paths and Knowledge Representation

Overview: Graph RAG systems can create dynamic, personalized learning experiences by representing knowledge and user progress as a graph.

Graph Structure:

1. **Nodes**:

   o Represent concepts, topics, or learning resources.

   o Example: Algebra, Calculus, Video123.

2. **Edges**:

   o Show relationships such as prerequisites or dependencies.

- Example:
  - Algebra → IS_PREREQUISITE_FOR → Calculus.

Workflow:

1. Query graph for prerequisites.

2. Suggest a learning path based on user progress.

Example:

- **Cypher Query**:

cypher

```cypher
MATCH (c:Concept)-[:IS_PREREQUISITE_FOR]->(next:Concept)
WHERE c.name = "Algebra"
RETURN next.name
```

- **Python Integration**:

python

```python
from transformers import pipeline

# Mock graph results
prerequisites = ["Algebra", "Trigonometry"]

# LLM for learning path generation
generator = pipeline("text-generation", model="gpt-3.5")
prompt = f"To master Calculus, start with:\n- {prerequisites[0]}\n-
{prerequisites[1]}.\nWhat is the best learning strategy?"
response = generator(prompt, max_length=150)
print(response[0]["generated_text"])
```

Output:

plaintext

To master Calculus, begin with Algebra to understand foundational equations, followed by Trigonometry for angle-based concepts.

10.7 Practice Problem: Designing a Knowledge-Driven Recommendation System

Problem Statement

Design a system that recommends books based on user preferences and graph data.

Steps to Solve

1. **Create the Knowledge Graph**:

   o Nodes: User, Book, Genre.

   o Edges: LIKES, BELONGS_TO.

Cypher Example:

cypher

```
CREATE (:User {name: "Alice"})
CREATE (:Book {title: "The Great Gatsby", genre: "Fiction"})
CREATE (:Genre {name: "Fiction"})
CREATE (:Genre {name: "Non-Fiction"})
CREATE (:Book {title: "Sapiens", genre: "Non-Fiction"})
CREATE (:User {name: "Bob"})
CREATE (:Book {title: "1984", genre: "Fiction"})
MATCH (b:Book), (g:Genre)
```

```cypher
WHERE b.genre = g.name
CREATE (b)-[:BELONGS_TO]->(g)
MATCH (u:User {name: "Alice"}), (b:Book {title: "The Great Gatsby"})
CREATE (u)-[:LIKES]->(b)
```

2. **Query the Graph**:

   o Recommend books in genres liked by the user.

Cypher Query:

cypher

```cypher
MATCH (u:User {name: "Alice"})-[:LIKES]->(b:Book)-
[:BELONGS_TO]->(g:Genre)<-[:BELONGS_TO]-(rec:Book)
WHERE NOT (u)-[:LIKES]->(rec)
RETURN rec.title
```

3. **Integrate with LLM**:

   • **Python Code**:

python

```python
from neo4j import GraphDatabase
from transformers import pipeline

class RecommendationSystem:
    def __init__(self, uri, user, password):
        self.driver = GraphDatabase.driver(uri, auth=(user, password))

    def close(self):
        self.driver.close()
```

```python
def recommend_books(self, username):
    query = """
    MATCH (u:User {name: $name})-[:LIKES]->(b:Book)-
[:BELONGS_TO]->(g:Genre)<-[:BELONGS_TO]-(rec:Book)
    WHERE NOT (u)-[:LIKES]->(rec)
    RETURN rec.title AS title
    """
    with self.driver.session() as session:
        results = session.run(query, name=username)
        return [record["title"] for record in results]

# Instantiate and get recommendations
recommendation_system =
RecommendationSystem("bolt://localhost:7687", "neo4j", "password")
recommendations = recommendation_system.recommend_books("Alice")

# LLM for explanations
generator = pipeline("text-generation", model="gpt-3.5")
prompt = f"Based on Alice's preferences, recommend:\n-
{recommendations[0]}"
response = generator(prompt, max_length=150)
print(response[0]["generated_text"])
recommendation_system.close()
```

Output:

plaintext

Based on Alice's preference for Fiction, we recommend "1984" for its compelling narrative and genre relevance.

Summary

1. **Scientific Discovery**:

- Multi-hop reasoning in graphs supports hypothesis generation.

2. **Conversational AI**:

   - Leverage graphs for detailed, context-aware chatbot responses.

3. **Educational Technology**:

   - Graphs enable personalized learning paths and concept tracking.

4. **Practice Problem**:

   - Hands-on example demonstrates the integration of graph data and LLMs in a recommendation system.

Chapter 11: Ethical and Practical Considerations

The implementation of Graph RAG (Retrieval-Augmented Generation) systems, while innovative and powerful, requires careful attention to ethical and practical considerations. This chapter explores critical areas, including data privacy, biases, and explainability.

11.1 Data Privacy and Security

11.1.1 Importance of Data Privacy and Security

1. **User Trust**:

     o   Ensuring data privacy builds trust among users.

     o   Example: Healthcare systems must protect sensitive patient data.

2. **Regulatory Compliance**:

     o   Adhering to laws such as GDPR, HIPAA, and CCPA is mandatory for organizations handling user data.

3. **Risk Mitigation**:

     o   Secure systems reduce the risk of data breaches and associated reputational damage.

11.1.2 Security Challenges in Graph RAG Systems

1. **Unauthorized Access**:

     o   Graphs often store sensitive information. Inadequate access controls can lead to data exposure.

o Example: Financial records in a graph database accessed without authorization.

2. **Data Leakage**:

o During LLM integration, unsecured communication channels may expose sensitive data.

3. **Inference Attacks**:

o Attackers may infer private information from accessible graph data.

11.1.3 Best Practices for Privacy and Security

1. **Access Control**:

o Implement role-based access controls (RBAC) to restrict access.

o **Neo4j Example**:

cypher

```
CALL dbms.security.createRole('medical_user')
CALL dbms.security.addUserToRole('john_doe', 'medical_user')
```

2. **Data Encryption**:

o Encrypt data at rest and in transit.

o Example: Use HTTPS for API communication.

3. **Anonymization**:

o Remove personally identifiable information (PII) from datasets.

o Example:

▪ Original: {name: "John Doe", age: 35}

▪ Anonymized: {user_id: "12345", age: 35}

4. **Audit Logs**:

- o   Maintain logs for all system access and modifications.

5. **Secured Integration with LLMs**:

    - o   Use secure APIs for data transfer.

    - o   Example: OAuth 2.0 for authentication.

11.1.4 Case Study: Healthcare Data Privacy

A Graph RAG system for symptom diagnosis stores sensitive medical records. To ensure privacy:

1. **Access Control**: Allow only authenticated doctors to query patient data.

2. **Encryption**: Use AES-256 encryption for all graph data.

3. **Anonymization**: Replace patient names with unique IDs.

11.2 Bias in Knowledge Graphs and LLM Integration

11.2.1 Sources of Bias

1. **Data Collection Bias**:

    - o   Graphs built from biased datasets inherit those biases.

    - o   Example: Over-representation of certain demographics in healthcare data.

2. **Model Bias**:

    - o   LLMs trained on biased text data may reinforce stereotypes.

3. **Graph Structure Bias**:

    - o   Central nodes (highly connected) may disproportionately influence results.

11.2.2 Consequences of Bias

1. **Unfair Recommendations**:

   o Example: A recommendation system favoring a specific demographic.

2. **Misinformation**:

   o Incorrect connections in graphs can propagate through LLM-generated content.

3. **Loss of Trust**:

   o Users may distrust systems perceived as biased.

11.2.3 Mitigation Strategies

1. **Diverse Data Sources**:

   o Build graphs from varied and representative datasets.

2. **Bias Detection Tools**:

   o Use algorithms to identify and correct bias in graphs.

   o Example: Compare node centrality metrics across demographics.

3. **Fair Querying**:

   o Design queries that balance results.

   o **Cypher Example**:

cypher

```
MATCH (u:User)-[:PURCHASED]->(p:Product)
WHERE u.age > 30
RETURN p.name, COUNT(*) AS purchases
ORDER BY purchases DESC
LIMIT 10
```

4. **Bias Audits for LLMs**:

- o Test LLM responses for stereotypical patterns.

11.2.4 Case Study: Reducing Bias in Healthcare Graphs

A healthcare graph over-represents data from urban hospitals. To address this:

1. Integrate rural health data.

2. Adjust weights in queries to prioritize underserved areas.

11.3 Ensuring Explainability in Graph RAG Systems

11.3.1 Importance of Explainability

1. **User Trust**:

   - o Transparent systems gain user confidence.

   - o Example: A user trusts a legal research tool that explains why a case was recommended.

2. **Debugging**:

   - o Explainability helps developers identify errors.

3. **Regulatory Requirements**:

   - o Laws like GDPR require explainable AI systems.

11.3.2 Methods for Explainability

1. **Graph Visualization**:

   - o Show relationships between nodes to explain query results.

   - o Tools: Neo4j Bloom, Gephi.

2. **Path Tracing**:

- o Trace the reasoning path in multi-hop queries.
- o **Cypher Example**:

cypher

```
MATCH p = (d:Disease)-[:HAS_SYMPTOM]->(:Symptom)
RETURN p
```

3. **LLM Explanation Generation**:
   - o Use LLMs to convert graph outputs into human-readable explanations.
   - o **Python Example**:

python

```python
from transformers import pipeline

# Mock graph results
path = "COVID-19 → Fever"
generator = pipeline("text-generation", model="gpt-3.5")
prompt = f"Explain the connection: {path}."
response = generator(prompt, max_length=100)
print(response[0]["generated_text"])
```

Output:

plaintext

COVID-19 is associated with Fever as a primary symptom based on medical observations.

4. **Confidence Scores**:
   - o Include scores for recommendations to indicate reliability.

11.3.3 Case Study: Explainability in Legal Research

A Graph RAG system for legal research provides:

1. **Graph Visualization**: Displays how a case is connected to precedents.

2. **LLM Summary**:

   o   Input: Graph query result.

   o   Output: "This case is cited in XYZ for its interpretation of contract law."

Summary

1. **Data Privacy and Security**:

   o   Use encryption, access control, and anonymization to protect user data.

2. **Bias in Graphs and LLMs**:

   o   Employ diverse data sources and bias detection tools to mitigate bias.

3. **Explainability**:

   o   Enhance transparency with graph visualizations, path tracing, and LLM explanations.

11.4 Responsible AI with Knowledge Graphs

11.4.1 Defining Responsible AI

Responsible AI ensures that AI systems, including those powered by Graph RAG, are designed and deployed ethically, transparently, and without harm. It encompasses fairness, accountability, transparency, and social benefit.

178

11.4.2 Principles of Responsible AI for Knowledge Graphs

1. **Fairness**:
   - Ensure equitable outcomes by addressing bias in graph construction and LLM integration.
   - Example: Avoiding over-representation of one demographic in healthcare graphs.

2. **Transparency**:
   - Make graph structures, queries, and LLM-generated outputs interpretable.
   - Example: Show the reasoning path in a recommendation system.

3. **Accountability**:
   - Enable auditing of graph data and LLM decisions.
   - Example: Maintain logs of graph modifications and LLM usage.

4. **Inclusivity**:
   - Include diverse stakeholders in graph design and validation.

5. **Sustainability**:
   - Minimize the environmental impact of training and querying large graphs and LLMs.

11.4.3 Implementing Responsible AI in Graph RAG Systems

1. **Ethical Graph Construction**:
   - Collect data from reliable and diverse sources.
   - Validate relationships to avoid misinformation.

2. **Explainable Outputs**:

- Generate user-friendly explanations for graph-based reasoning and LLM outputs.
- Example: Use path tracing to explain disease diagnoses.

3. **Regular Audits**:
   - Periodically review graph data and LLM behaviors to ensure alignment with ethical standards.

4. **Feedback Loops**:
   - Collect user feedback to improve system fairness and usability.

11.4.4 Example: Ethical Recommendations in E-Commerce

A Graph RAG system avoids unfair biases in product recommendations by:

1. Balancing query results using demographic filters.
2. Displaying reasoning paths for recommendations.

Example Cypher Query:

cypher

```
MATCH (u:User)-[:LIKES]->(p:Product)-[:SIMILAR_TO]-
>(rec:Product)
WHERE NOT (u)-[:LIKES]->(rec) AND rec.price <= $budget
RETURN rec.name
```

11.5 Ethical Concerns in Real-World Deployments

11.5.1 Ethical Concerns

1. **Privacy Violations**:
   - Unauthorized use of sensitive graph data.
   - Example: Sharing medical graph insights without patient consent.

2. **Bias and Discrimination**:
   - Over-representation or omission of certain groups in graph data.
   - Example: An education graph favoring urban students over rural ones.

3. **Misinformation**:
   - Incorrect or outdated relationships in graphs.
   - Example: A knowledge graph linking "COVID-19" to disproven treatments.

4. **Lack of Accountability**:
   - Difficulty tracing decisions made by integrated Graph RAG systems.

11.5.2 Addressing Ethical Concerns

1. **Informed Consent**:
   - Ensure users understand how their data is used.
   - Example: Explicitly disclose data usage in healthcare applications.

2. **Graph Validation**:
   - Validate relationships before deployment to prevent misinformation.

3. **Algorithmic Fairness**:
   - Use algorithms that balance outputs across different groups.

- o **Example in Python**:

python

```
def balance_results(results, demographic_field):
    demographics = {r[demographic_field] for r in results}
    return [r for r in results if r[demographic_field] in demographics]
```

4. **Redress Mechanisms**:

- o Provide users with ways to challenge and correct outputs.

11.5.3 Example: Avoiding Misinformation in Legal Graphs

A legal knowledge graph ensures accuracy by:

1. Cross-referencing with official legal databases.

2. Periodically updating case relationships.

Validation Query:

cypher

```
MATCH (c:Case)-[:MENTIONS]->(l:Law)
WHERE NOT EXISTS {
    MATCH (db:LegalDatabase {verified: true})-[:HAS]->(c)
}
RETURN c.name
```

11.6 Case Study: Bias Mitigation in Healthcare Knowledge Graphs

---

11.6.1 Background

Healthcare knowledge graphs often exhibit biases due to:

1. Unequal representation of demographic groups.

2. Data skewed toward urban healthcare providers.

Problem: A healthcare graph disproportionately links diseases to symptoms common in urban areas, ignoring rural-specific conditions.

11.6.2 Approach to Bias Mitigation

1. **Expand Data Sources**:

   o Include rural healthcare datasets.

   o Example: Collect disease incidence data from community health workers.

2. **Weight Adjustments**:

   o Assign higher weights to underrepresented nodes or edges.

   o **Cypher Query**:

cypher

```
MATCH (d:Disease)-[r:HAS_SYMPTOM]->(s:Symptom)
WHERE d.region = "Rural"
SET r.weight = r.weight * 1.5
```

3. **Graph Audits**:

   o Regularly assess node and edge distributions.

   o Example: Ensure even distribution of symptoms across regions.

11.6.3 Implementation

Scenario: A Graph RAG system predicts diseases based on symptoms. Without intervention, it over-predicts urban diseases.

Mitigation Steps:

1. **Reweight Edges**:
   - o   Adjust weights to favor rural disease relationships.

2. **Evaluate Outputs**:
   - o   Test predictions on rural test datasets.

3. **User Feedback**:
   - o   Collect feedback from rural healthcare workers to refine predictions.

11.6.4 Results

After bias mitigation:

1. **Improved Accuracy**:
   - o   The system correctly associates rural-specific diseases with symptoms.

2. **Enhanced Trust**:
   - o   Rural healthcare providers report increased satisfaction with the system.

11.6.5 Python Implementation: Bias Detection

python

```
def detect_bias(graph_data, attribute):
    counts = {}
    for node in graph_data:
        counts[node[attribute]] = counts.get(node[attribute], 0) + 1
    return counts

# Example graph data
```

```
graph_data = [{"region": "Urban"}, {"region": "Urban"}, {"region": "Rural"}]

# Detect bias in node distribution
bias_report = detect_bias(graph_data, "region")
print(bias_report)
```

Output:

plaintext

```
{'Urban': 2, 'Rural': 1}
```

Summary

1. **Responsible AI**:
   - o   Implement fairness, transparency, and sustainability in Graph RAG systems.

2. **Ethical Concerns**:
   - o   Address privacy, bias, and misinformation through informed consent and validation.

3. **Bias Mitigation Case Study**:
   - o   Demonstrates how to reduce bias in a healthcare graph, improving accuracy and inclusivity.

Chapter 12: Challenges and Solutions in Graph RAG

Graph RAG (Retrieval-Augmented Generation) systems are powerful but complex, and building them presents several challenges. This chapter discusses common pitfalls, solutions for handling noisy or incomplete data, and strategies to reduce computational overhead.

12.1 Common Pitfalls in Building Knowledge Graphs

12.1.1 Inaccurate or Misleading Relationships

- **Problem**: Incorrect edges in the graph can lead to unreliable outputs.

  - Example: Linking "COVID-19" to a disproven treatment.

- **Solution**:

1. **Validation Tools**:

   - Use validation rules or algorithms to detect and correct anomalies.

2. **Domain Experts**:

   - Collaborate with experts to vet relationships.

Code Example:

cypher

```
MATCH (d:Disease)-[r:HAS_TREATMENT]->(t:Treatment)
WHERE t.approved_by IS NULL
RETURN r
```

12.1.2 Overcomplication

- **Problem**: Overly complex graphs with redundant nodes and edges reduce efficiency.

    o Example: Multiple nodes representing the same entity due to inconsistent naming.

- **Solution**:

1. **Normalization**:

    - Merge duplicate nodes based on attributes.

2. **Simplification**:

    - Focus on essential relationships for your use case.

Cypher Query for Normalization:

cypher

```
MATCH (n1:Node), (n2:Node)
WHERE n1.name = n2.name AND ID(n1) <> ID(n2)
MERGE (n1)-[:MERGED]->(n2)
```

12.1.3 Lack of Scalability

- **Problem**: Small-scale graphs fail to handle real-world data growth.

- **Solution**:

    1. Use scalable databases like Neo4j Enterprise or Amazon Neptune.

    2. Optimize queries for large-scale graphs.

12.2 Dealing with Noisy or Incomplete Data

12.2.1 Identifying Noise

- **Problem**: Noisy data introduces irrelevant or misleading nodes and edges.

    o Example: Social media text added as-is to a knowledge graph.

- **Solution**:

1. **Filters**:

    - Apply rules to discard irrelevant or low-quality data.

2. **Statistical Metrics**:

    - Identify anomalies using metrics like outliers or low centrality.

Python Example: Filtering Noisy Nodes:

python

```python
def filter_noisy_nodes(graph_data, threshold):
    return [node for node in graph_data if node['relevance_score'] >
threshold]

# Example Data
nodes = [{"name": "Node1", "relevance_score": 0.9}, {"name": "Node2",
"relevance_score": 0.2}]
filtered_nodes = filter_noisy_nodes(nodes, 0.5)
print(filtered_nodes)
```
Output:

plaintext

[{'name': 'Node1', 'relevance_score': 0.9}]

12.2.2 Completing Incomplete Graphs

- **Problem**: Missing nodes or edges lead to incomplete reasoning paths.

  - o Example: A disease node missing symptoms.

- **Solution**:

1. **Data Augmentation**:

   - Add missing data from external sources or datasets.

2. **Machine Learning**:

   - Use graph embeddings or GNNs to predict missing edges.

Code Example: Predicting Missing Edges with PyTorch Geometric:

python

```python
import torch
from torch_geometric.nn import GCNConv

class EdgePredictor(torch.nn.Module):
    def __init__(self):
        super().__init__()
        self.conv1 = GCNConv(16, 32)
        self.conv2 = GCNConv(32, 16)

    def forward(self, x, edge_index):
        x = self.conv1(x, edge_index)
```

```
x = self.conv2(x, edge_index)
return x

# Predict missing edges using a trained model
# Input: Node features and existing edges
```

12.2.3 Validation

- Regularly validate graph data to remove outdated or irrelevant entries.

Validation Query:

cypher

```
MATCH (n)-[r]->(m)
WHERE r.created_date < date() - duration({days: 365})
DELETE r
```

12.3 Reducing Computational Overhead

12.3.1 Challenges

1. **Expensive Queries:**

   o Example: Multi-hop queries on large graphs.

2. **High Memory Usage:**

   o Example: Loading the entire graph into memory for analysis.

12.3.2 Optimization Techniques

1. **Indexing:**

- Speed up queries by indexing key properties.
- **Example**:

cypher

```
CREATE INDEX ON :Disease(name)
```

2. **Query Optimization**:
   - Minimize traversal depth and use constraints.
   - **Example**:

cypher

```
MATCH (d:Disease)-[:HAS_SYMPTOM]->(s:Symptom)
WHERE d.name = "COVID-19" AND s.relevance > 0.8
RETURN s.name
```

3. **Partitioning**:
   - Divide large graphs into smaller subgraphs for parallel processing.

12.3.3 Caching

- Cache frequently accessed subgraphs or results.
- **Python Example**:

python

```
from cachetools import cached, LRUCache

cache = LRUCache(maxsize=100)

@cached(cache)
def query_graph(node):
    # Simulate a graph query
```

```
    return f"Results for {node}"

print(query_graph("COVID-19"))
```

12.3.4 Distributed Systems

- Use distributed graph databases like TigerGraph or Amazon Neptune for horizontal scaling.

12.3.5 Example: Parallel Query Execution

Python Code:

python

```
from concurrent.futures import ThreadPoolExecutor

def execute_query(query):
    # Simulated query execution
    return f"Results for {query}"

queries = ["Query1", "Query2", "Query3"]
with ThreadPoolExecutor() as executor:
    results = list(executor.map(execute_query, queries))
print(results)
```

Output:

plaintext

```
['Results for Query1', 'Results for Query2', 'Results for Query3']
```

Summary

1. **Common Pitfalls**:

- Address inaccuracies, overcomplications, and scalability issues in graph design.

2. **Noisy and Incomplete Data**:

   - Use filtering, augmentation, and machine learning to handle data quality issues.

3. **Reducing Computational Overhead**:

   - Apply indexing, caching, and distributed systems to optimize performance.

12.4 Debugging Graph Retrieval Systems

Debugging graph retrieval systems involves identifying issues in queries, graph structures, and integrations with downstream systems like LLMs.

12.4.1 Common Issues in Graph Retrieval

1. **Incorrect Query Results**:

   - Mismatched results due to syntax errors or faulty logic in queries.

   - Example: A query retrieves all nodes instead of filtering by specific attributes.

2. **Performance Bottlenecks**:

   - Long-running queries caused by inefficient traversal logic.

   - Example: Multi-hop queries on unindexed graphs.

3. **Integration Failures**:

   - Mismatches between graph outputs and the requirements of downstream LLMs.

   - Example: Missing or improperly formatted graph data for LLM prompts.

4. **Concurrency Issues**:

o Errors when multiple queries run simultaneously on the same database.

12.4.2 Debugging Techniques

1. **Query Profiling**:

    o Use profiling tools to identify inefficiencies in graph queries.

    o **Example in Neo4j**:

cypher

PROFILE MATCH (n:Node)-[:RELATES_TO]->(m:Node)
RETURN n, m

2. **Stepwise Execution**:

    o Break complex queries into smaller parts to isolate errors.

    o Example:

        1. Retrieve nodes first.

        2. Test edges independently.

3. **Error Logs**:

    o Check database logs for errors or warnings.

4. **Test Cases**:

    o Create unit tests for individual queries to ensure correctness.

12.4.3 Debugging Example

Faulty Query:

cypher

```
MATCH (d:Disease)-[:HAS_SYMPTOM]->(s:Symptom)
WHERE s.name = "Fever" OR d.name = "COVID-19"
RETURN d.name
```

Issue:

- Retrieves diseases unrelated to "Fever" because of the OR logic.

Corrected Query:

cypher

```
MATCH (d:Disease)-[:HAS_SYMPTOM]->(s:Symptom)
WHERE s.name = "Fever"
RETURN d.name
UNION
MATCH (d:Disease)
WHERE d.name = "COVID-19"
RETURN d.name
```

12.5 Ensuring Robustness in Large-Scale Applications

12.5.1 Challenges in Large-Scale Applications

1. **High Data Volume**:

   o Large graphs with millions of nodes and edges require efficient processing.

2. **Concurrency Management**:

   o Multiple users querying the graph simultaneously can lead to contention.

3. **Data Consistency**:

- o Maintaining consistent graph states during frequent updates.

4. **Fault Tolerance**:

    - o Systems must recover gracefully from failures.

12.5.2 Strategies for Robustness

1. **Scaling Infrastructure**:

    - o Use distributed databases for horizontal scalability.

    - o Example: Amazon Neptune or TigerGraph for enterprise-grade applications.

2. **Indexing**:

    - o Index frequently queried attributes for faster lookups.

    - o **Example**:

cypher

```
CREATE INDEX ON :Symptom(name)
```

3. **Caching**:

    - o Cache frequently accessed subgraphs or query results to reduce database load.

4. **Redundancy**:

    - o Use replication to ensure high availability.

    - o Example: Neo4j Enterprise supports multi-cluster deployments.

5. **Stress Testing**:

    - o Simulate high query loads to evaluate system performance.

6. **Monitoring Tools**:

o Use tools like Prometheus or Grafana to track query times, error rates, and resource usage.

12.5.3 Example: Handling Concurrency

Problem: Two users attempt to update the same edge simultaneously.

Solution:

1. **Use Transactions**:

cypher

```
BEGIN
MATCH (d:Disease {name: "COVID-19"})-[r:HAS_SYMPTOM]-
>(s:Symptom {name: "Fever"})
SET r.weight = 1.5
COMMIT
```

2. **Lock Mechanisms**:

o Ensure updates are serialized.

12.6 Practice Problem: Debugging and Optimizing Graph Queries

---

Problem Statement

You manage a Graph RAG system for an e-commerce platform. A query designed to recommend products based on user preferences runs slowly and occasionally returns irrelevant results.

Task

1. Debug the query for accuracy.

2. Optimize its performance for large-scale usage.

Graph Data

Node	Attributes	Edges
User1	{age: 30}	PURCHASED → ProductA
ProductA	{category: "Phone"}	SIMILAR_TO → ProductB
ProductB	{category: "Phone"}	SIMILAR_TO → ProductC

Initial Query

cypher

```
MATCH (u:User {name: "User1"})-[:PURCHASED]->(p:Product)-
[:SIMILAR_TO]->(rec:Product)
RETURN rec.name
```

Debugging

1. **Check Results**:

   o Query returns products unrelated to User1's preferences due to missing filters.

2. **Add Filters**:

   o Restrict results to products in the same category.

cypher

```
MATCH (u:User {name: "User1"})-[:PURCHASED]->(p:Product)-
[:SIMILAR_TO]->(rec:Product)
WHERE rec.category = p.category
RETURN rec.name
```

Optimization

1. **Add Index**:

   o Index the category property for faster filtering.

cypher

CREATE INDEX ON :Product(category)

2. **Limit Results**:

   o Retrieve only the top 5 recommendations.

cypher

RETURN rec.name LIMIT 5

3. **Profile Query**:

   o Analyze performance.

cypher

```
PROFILE MATCH (u:User {name: "User1"})-[:PURCHASED]-
>(p:Product)-[:SIMILAR_TO]->(rec:Product)
RETURN rec.name
```

Python Integration

python

```python
from neo4j import GraphDatabase

class GraphQueryOptimizer:
    def __init__(self, uri, user, password):
        self.driver = GraphDatabase.driver(uri, auth=(user, password))

    def close(self):
        self.driver.close()
```

```python
def recommend_products(self, username):
    query = """
    MATCH (u:User {name: $name})-[:PURCHASED]->(p:Product)-
    [:SIMILAR_TO]->(rec:Product)
    WHERE rec.category = p.category
    RETURN rec.name LIMIT 5
    """
    with self.driver.session() as session:
        results = session.run(query, name=username)
        return [record["rec.name"] for record in results]

# Use the optimized query
optimizer = GraphQueryOptimizer("bolt://localhost:7687", "neo4j",
"password")
recommendations = optimizer.recommend_products("User1")
print("Recommendations:", recommendations)
optimizer.close()
```

Expected Output

plaintext

Recommendations: ['ProductB', 'ProductC']

Summary

1. **Debugging**:
   - Profile queries, break them into smaller parts, and validate results.

2. **Robustness**:
   - Ensure scalability, concurrency management, and fault tolerance.

3. **Practice Problem**:

- Demonstrated a step-by-step approach to debugging and optimizing a graph query for real-world scenarios.

Chapter 13: Case Studies and Real-World Implementations

This chapter highlights real-world applications of Graph RAG (Retrieval-Augmented Generation) systems. We explore three major case studies: enterprise knowledge management, e-commerce product recommendations, and advanced search engines powered by Graph RAG.

13.1 Enterprise Knowledge Management with Graph RAG

Overview

Organizations often struggle to manage large volumes of internal data scattered across documents, databases, and systems. Graph RAG systems enable enterprises to structure their knowledge and make it accessible for decision-making and operational efficiency.

Implementation Steps

1. **Knowledge Graph Creation**:

   o   Nodes: Document, Employee, Project, Department.

   o   Edges: AUTHOR_OF, BELONGS_TO, WORKS_ON.

Example Graph Data:

Node	Attributes	Edges
Document1	{title: "Report A"}	AUTHOR_OF → Employee1
Employee1	{name: "Alice"}	BELONGS_TO → Department1

Node	Attributes	Edges
Project1	{name: "Project X"}	WORKS_ON → Employee1

2. **Data Integration**:

   o Aggregate data from sources like internal wikis, SharePoint, and email archives.

3. **Query System**:

   o Employees query the graph for specific information.

Example Query:

cypher

```cypher
MATCH (e:Employee)-[:AUTHOR_OF]->(d:Document)
WHERE e.name = "Alice"
RETURN d.title
```

4. **LLM Integration**:

   o Combine retrieved data with LLMs to generate contextual responses.

Example Use Case

Scenario: An employee wants to find all reports authored by colleagues working on "Project X."

Python Integration:

python

```python
from neo4j import GraphDatabase
from transformers import pipeline

class KnowledgeQuery:
    def __init__(self, uri, user, password):
```

```python
        self.driver = GraphDatabase.driver(uri, auth=(user, password))

    def close(self):
        self.driver.close()

    def query_reports(self, project_name):
        query = """
        MATCH (p:Project {name: $name})<-[:WORKS_ON]-
(e:Employee)-[:AUTHOR_OF]->(d:Document)
        RETURN d.title AS title, e.name AS author
        """
        with self.driver.session() as session:
            results = session.run(query, name=project_name)
            return [{"title": record["title"], "author": record["author"]} for
record in results]

# Query and summarize
knowledge_query = KnowledgeQuery("bolt://localhost:7687", "neo4j",
"password")
reports = knowledge_query.query_reports("Project X")
generator = pipeline("text-generation", model="gpt-3.5")
prompt = f"Summarize the following reports:\n{reports}"
response = generator(prompt, max_length=200)
print(response[0]["generated_text"])
knowledge_query.close()
```

Output:

plaintext

Reports authored by employees working on Project X include
"Report A" by Alice. These documents provide insights into project
deliverables.

13.2 E-Commerce Product Recommendations

Overview

E-commerce platforms rely on recommendation systems to enhance user experience and increase sales. Graph RAG systems enable more accurate and personalized recommendations by integrating structured product data with user preferences.

Implementation Steps

1. **Graph Structure**:

   o Nodes: User, Product, Category.

   o Edges: PURCHASED, VIEWED, SIMILAR_TO.

Example Graph Data:

Node	Attributes	Edges
User1	{age: 25}	PURCHASED → ProductA
ProductA	{category: "Phone"}	SIMILAR_TO → ProductB

2. **Query System**:

   o Retrieve recommendations based on user purchase history.

Example Query:

cypher

```
MATCH (u:User {name: "User1"})-[:PURCHASED]->(p:Product)-
[:SIMILAR_TO]->(rec:Product)
RETURN rec.name
```

3. **Personalization**:

- o Use LLMs to tailor recommendations to individual preferences.

Example Use Case

Scenario: A user browses smartphones. The system suggests accessories and complementary products.

Python Integration:

python

```
from transformers import pipeline

# Mock data
recommendations = [{"name": "Smartphone Case"}, {"name": "Wireless Charger"}]

# LLM explanation
generator = pipeline("text-generation", model="gpt-3.5")
prompt = f"User browsed smartphones. Recommended products:\n-
{recommendations[0]['name']}\n- {recommendations[1]['name']}.\nWhy
are these products suitable?"
response = generator(prompt, max_length=150)
print(response[0]["generated_text"])
```

Output:

plaintext

Based on the user's interest in smartphones, accessories like a Smartphone Case and a Wireless Charger are recommended for protection and convenience.

13.3 Advanced Search Engines Powered by Graph RAG

Overview

Search engines powered by Graph RAG go beyond keyword matching by integrating knowledge graphs and LLMs to deliver contextual and precise results.

Implementation Steps

1. **Graph Construction**:

   o   Nodes: Topic, Document, Author.

   o   Edges: MENTIONS, WRITTEN_BY.

Example Graph Data:

Node	Attributes	Edges
Topic1	{name: "AI"}	MENTIONS → Document1
Document1	{title: "AI Basics"}	WRITTEN_BY → Author1

2. **Query System**:

   o   Retrieve documents and related topics based on user queries.

Example Query:

cypher

```
MATCH (t:Topic {name: "AI"})-[:MENTIONS]->(d:Document)
RETURN d.title
```

3. **LLM Integration**:

- o   Summarize results and suggest related topics.

Example Use Case

Scenario: A user searches for "AI applications." The system retrieves documents and suggests related areas.

Python Integration:

python

```
# Mock data
results = [{"title": "AI in Healthcare"}, {"title": "AI in Finance"}]

# LLM summarization
prompt = f"User searched for AI applications. Retrieved documents:\n-
{results[0]['title']}\n- {results[1]['title']}.\nSummarize and suggest related
topics."
response = pipeline("text-generation", model="gpt-3.5")(prompt,
max_length=200)
print(response[0]["generated_text"])
```

Output:

plaintext

Documents on AI applications include "AI in Healthcare" and "AI in Finance." Related topics may include AI ethics and AI in education.

Summary

1. **Enterprise Knowledge Management**:
    - o   Graph RAG simplifies access to internal knowledge and improves decision-making.

2. **E-Commerce**:

   o Personalized product recommendations enhance user satisfaction and sales.

3. **Advanced Search Engines**:

   o Graph RAG delivers precise, contextual results and suggests related topics.

These real-world case studies demonstrate the versatility and impact of Graph RAG systems across industries. The next chapter will discuss the future directions and advancements in Graph RAG technology.

14.4 The Role of Open Knowledge Graphs in AI Systems

14.4.1 What Are Open Knowledge Graphs?

Open Knowledge Graphs (OKGs) are publicly accessible datasets that represent structured knowledge through nodes (entities) and edges (relationships). Examples include Wikidata, DBpedia, and Freebase. These resources provide a foundation for AI systems to retrieve, reason, and generate contextually rich responses.

14.4.2 Importance of Open Knowledge Graphs in AI

1. **Accessible and Scalable Knowledge Base**:

   o OKGs provide a vast and continuously updated repository of general and domain-specific knowledge.

   o Example: Wikidata contains millions of entities across diverse domains.

2. **Interoperability**:

   o Open standards like RDF (Resource Description Framework) enable seamless integration with AI systems.

3. **Community-Driven Updates**:

   o Contributions from global communities ensure that OKGs remain up-to-date and cover emerging topics.

4. **Cost-Effectiveness**:

   o Free and open access reduces the cost of building proprietary knowledge bases.

14.4.3 Use Cases in AI Systems

1. **Question Answering**:

   o AI models use OKGs for fact-based answers.

   o **Example**:

      ▪ Question: "Who is the president of France?"

      ▪ Query:

sparql

```
SELECT ?president WHERE {
 ?person wdt:P31 wd:Q5;
     wdt:P39 wd:Q11613.
}
```

2. **Recommendation Systems**:

   o Enhance product or content recommendations using linked data.

   o Example: Suggesting books by the same author using author relationships.

3. **Natural Language Generation (NLG)**:

   o OKGs provide structured facts for generating coherent and accurate responses.

14.4.4 Challenges in Using OKGs

1. **Data Quality**:

   o Incomplete or incorrect data can impact AI outputs.

2. **Scalability**:

   o Large-scale OKGs require efficient querying and integration.

3. **Bias**:

   o OKGs may reflect biases inherent in their sources.

14.4.5 Example: Integrating Open Knowledge Graphs in AI

Scenario: Build a chatbot that uses Wikidata to answer factual questions.

Implementation Steps:

1. Query Wikidata using SPARQL.

2. Format the retrieved data for input to an LLM.

3. Use the LLM to generate user-friendly responses.

Python Example:

python

```
from SPARQLWrapper import SPARQLWrapper, JSON
from transformers import pipeline

# Query Wikidata
def query_wikidata(question):
    sparql = SPARQLWrapper("https://query.wikidata.org/sparql")
    sparql.setQuery("""
    SELECT ?presidentLabel WHERE {
      ?person wdt:P31 wd:Q5;
          wdt:P39 wd:Q11613.
```

```
    SERVICE wikibase:label { bd:serviceParam wikibase:language
"[AUTO_LANGUAGE],en". }
    }
    """)
    sparql.setReturnFormat(JSON)
    results = sparql.query().convert()
    return results["results"]["bindings"][0]["presidentLabel"]["value"]

# LLM Explanation
president = query_wikidata("Who is the president of France?")
generator = pipeline("text-generation", model="gpt-3.5")
prompt = f"The president of France is {president}. Provide more details."
response = generator(prompt, max_length=150)
print(response[0]["generated_text"])
```

Output:

plaintext

The president of France is Emmanuel Macron. He has been in office
since 2017 and is known for his progressive economic policies.

14.5 Predictions for Graph RAG in the Next Decade

14.5.1 Enhanced Integration with Large Language Models

1. **Dynamic Contextualization**:

   o LLMs will seamlessly integrate with graphs to provide
     context-aware and domain-specific responses.

   o Example: A medical assistant AI fetching patient
     histories from a graph during consultations.

2. **Autonomous Reasoning**:

- o Multi-hop reasoning capabilities will improve, enabling LLMs to simulate logical thinking.

14.5.2 Evolution of Knowledge Graphs

1. **Hybrid Graphs**:

   - o Combining traditional graphs with neural embeddings for richer representations.

2. **Real-Time Updates**:

   - o AI systems will process real-time streams to keep graphs current.

   - o Example: Updating graphs with live financial data for market predictions.

3. **Scalability**:

   - o Advances in distributed systems and cloud computing will enable graphs to scale to billions of entities and relationships.

14.5.3 Democratization of AI with Open Data

1. **Accessible AI Solutions**:

   - o Open Knowledge Graphs and free LLMs will empower small enterprises and developers to build sophisticated AI systems.

2. **Community-Driven Improvements**:

   - o Crowdsourced updates to OKGs will ensure diversity and accuracy.

14.5.4 Expansion of Applications

1. **Healthcare**:

- o Disease tracking and personalized medicine.
- o Example: Graph RAG assisting doctors in diagnosis by connecting symptoms, diseases, and treatments.

2. **Education**:
   - o Adaptive learning systems offering personalized study plans.
   - o Example: Graph RAG suggesting courses based on a student's performance and goals.

3. **Autonomous Systems**:
   - o Self-driving cars leveraging spatial knowledge graphs for navigation and decision-making.

14.5.5 Challenges and Opportunities

1. **Ethical Considerations**:
   - o Addressing biases, data privacy, and explainability in AI systems.

2. **Technical Barriers**:
   - o Optimizing performance and reducing computational costs for large-scale systems.

14.5.6 Vision for the Future

In the next decade, Graph RAG will be at the forefront of AI innovation, driving applications in healthcare, education, e-commerce, and more. Its combination of structured knowledge and generative capabilities will revolutionize human-AI interaction, making AI systems more reliable, scalable, and intelligent.

Summary

1. **Role of Open Knowledge Graphs**:

- OKGs like Wikidata are essential for scalable and cost-effective AI systems, offering accessible and structured knowledge.

2. **Future of Graph RAG**:

- Expect deeper LLM integration, real-time graph updates, and applications across diverse domains.

3. **Opportunities and Challenges**:

- Embrace advancements while addressing biases and technical barriers to ensure equitable and efficient systems.

13.4 Cross-Industry Collaboration Using Knowledge Graphs

13.4.1 Importance of Cross-Industry Collaboration

1. **Shared Knowledge Base**:

- Industries can benefit from shared knowledge, such as environmental data or global supply chains.

- Example: Healthcare and finance industries collaborating on patient financial assistance programs.

2. **Efficiency and Innovation**:

- Sharing resources accelerates innovation by reducing redundant efforts.

- Example: The automotive and telecommunications industries collaborating on vehicle-to-network (V2N) communication.

3. **Global Challenges**:

- Complex issues like climate change and pandemic response require collaborative knowledge sharing.

- Example: Governments and research institutions using knowledge graphs to track disease outbreaks.

13.4.2 Collaborative Knowledge Graph Structures

1. **Nodes and Edges**:

   - Nodes: Represent entities shared across industries, such as Company, Project, or Regulation.

   - Edges: Define relationships like COLLABORATES_WITH, REGULATED_BY, or USES_TECHNOLOGY.

2. **Example Knowledge Graph**:

Node	Attributes	Edges
CompanyA	{industry: "Healthcare"}	COLLABORATES_WITH → CompanyB
TechnologyX	{type: "AI Model"}	USED_BY → CompanyA

13.4.3 Use Cases

1. **Healthcare and AI**:

   - AI companies collaborating with healthcare providers to improve diagnostics.

   - Example: Sharing anonymized patient data to train disease detection models.

2. **Supply Chain Management**:

   - Industries like retail and logistics collaborating on global inventory tracking.

   - Example: A graph tracking goods from manufacturers to retailers.

3. **Research and Development**:

   o Universities and corporations working together to develop new technologies.

   o Example: A knowledge graph linking academic research to industry patents.

13.4.4 Example: Cross-Industry Graph Query

Scenario: A query identifies shared technologies between healthcare and automotive companies.

Cypher Query:

cypher

```
MATCH (c1:Company {industry: "Healthcare"})-
[:USES_TECHNOLOGY]->(t:Technology)<-[:USES_TECHNOLOGY]-
(c2:Company {industry: "Automotive"})
RETURN c1.name AS HealthcareCompany, c2.name AS
AutomotiveCompany, t.name AS Technology
```

Output:

Healthcare Company	Automotive Company	Technology
MediTech	AutoDrive	Machine Learning

13.4.5 Challenges

1. **Data Sharing Agreements**:

   o Collaborating parties must address privacy and ownership concerns.

2. **Interoperability**:

   o Ensuring data compatibility across industries.

3. **Security**:

   o   Protecting sensitive data in a collaborative
       environment.

13.4.6 Solutions

1. **Standardized Formats**:

   o   Use RDF or other open standards for data exchange.

2. **Access Control**:

   o   Implement role-based permissions for graph queries.

3. **Smart Contracts**:

   o   Blockchain technology can manage agreements for
       data usage.

13.5 Community Contributions and Open-Source Tools

13.5.1 Role of Open-Source Tools in Graph RAG

1. **Accessibility**:

   o   Open-source tools lower the barrier for developers
       and organizations to adopt Graph RAG.

2. **Collaboration**:

   o   Communities contribute to improving tools and
       resources.

3. **Innovation**:

   o   Open-source fosters experimentation and rapid
       iteration.

13.5.2 Popular Open-Source Tools for Knowledge Graphs

1. **Neo4j**:

   o Graph database for building and querying knowledge graphs.

   o Features: Cypher query language, visualization tools.

2. **RDFLib**:

   o Python library for creating and working with RDF data.

   o Features: SPARQL query support, data serialization.

3. **ArangoDB**:

   o Multi-model database with graph capabilities.

   o Features: AQL query language, scalability.

4. **GraphX (Apache Spark)**:

   o Framework for distributed graph processing.

   o Features: Integration with big data ecosystems.

13.5.3 Contribution Opportunities

1. **Developing Plugins**:

   o Extend tools like Neo4j with industry-specific functionality.

   o Example: A healthcare module for symptom-disease mappings.

2. **Data Contributions**:

   o Enrich open knowledge graphs like Wikidata with verified data.

3. **Documentation and Tutorials**:

- Create resources to help others learn and adopt Graph RAG systems.

13.5.4 Example: Using an Open-Source Tool

Scenario: Building a graph to manage academic research collaborations.

Python Example with RDFLib:

python

```
from rdflib import Graph, URIRef, Literal, Namespace

# Create a graph
g = Graph()

# Define namespaces
EX = Namespace("http://example.org/")
g.bind("ex", EX)

# Add data
g.add((URIRef(EX["Researcher1"]), EX["COLLABORATES_WITH"],
URIRef(EX["Researcher2"])))
g.add((URIRef(EX["Researcher1"]), EX["WORKS_ON"], Literal("AI
Research")))

# Query the graph
query = """
PREFIX ex: <http://example.org/>
SELECT ?researcher ?project
WHERE {
  ?researcher ex:WORKS_ON ?project.
}
"""

for row in g.query(query):
```

```python
print(f"Researcher: {row.researcher}, Project: {row.project}")
```

Output:

plaintext

Researcher: http://example.org/Researcher1, Project: AI Research

---

13.5.5 Benefits of Community Contributions

1. **Shared Resources**:

    o   Access to datasets, libraries, and frameworks.

2. **Collaborative Development**:

    o   Faster identification and resolution of bugs or limitations.

3. **Global Network**:

    o   Opportunities to collaborate with experts worldwide.

Summary

1. **Cross-Industry Collaboration**:

    o   Knowledge graphs enable industries to share data, improve efficiency, and innovate.

2. **Open-Source Tools**:

    o   Platforms like Neo4j and RDFLib drive Graph RAG adoption and accessibility.

3. **Community Contributions**:

    o   Open-source ecosystems thrive on collaborative efforts, benefiting all stakeholders.

These topics highlight how collaboration and community efforts can significantly enhance the development and adoption of Graph RAG systems. The next chapter will explore ethical considerations in deploying Graph RAG for diverse applications.

Chapter 14: Future Directions in Graph RAG and LLMs

As Graph RAG (Retrieval-Augmented Generation) systems evolve, their integration with large language models (LLMs) and knowledge graphs (KGs) will significantly impact AI applications. This chapter explores emerging trends in KG research, advances in LLM architectures for graph integration, and AI-driven methods for graph construction and expansion.

14.1 Emerging Trends in Knowledge Graph Research

14.1.1 Hybrid Knowledge Graphs

1. **Definition**:

   o Hybrid knowledge graphs combine symbolic representations (traditional graphs) with neural embeddings.

2. **Advantages**:

   o Improved reasoning by blending precise relationships with approximate, vector-based similarities.

3. **Example**:

   o A hybrid graph for healthcare could explicitly connect diseases and symptoms while embedding patient records for similarity-based predictions.

14.1.2 Temporal Knowledge Graphs

1. **Definition**:

- Graphs that incorporate time-based information for dynamic reasoning.

2. **Use Cases**:

- Tracking the progression of diseases or monitoring financial trends.

3. **Challenges**:

- Efficiently querying and updating temporal data.

Example Query for Temporal Graphs:

cypher

```
MATCH (event:Event)
WHERE event.timestamp >= "2023-01-01"
RETURN event.name, event.timestamp
```

14.1.3 Explainable Knowledge Graphs

1. **Definition**:

- Graphs designed to enhance explainability in AI by documenting reasoning paths.

2. **Example**:

- A knowledge graph that shows the steps leading to a recommendation, such as "Symptom X → Disease Y → Treatment Z."

14.1.4 Federated Knowledge Graphs

1. **Definition**:

- Federated graphs aggregate data from multiple sources while preserving data sovereignty.

2. **Applications**:

- o Healthcare systems sharing anonymized patient data across regions.

3. **Challenges**:

  - o Harmonizing data formats and ensuring security.

14.2 Advances in LLM Architectures for Graph Integration

14.2.1 Enhanced Attention Mechanisms

1. **Graph-Aware Attention**:

   - o Modify transformer architectures to focus on graph structures during input encoding.

2. **Benefits**:

   - o Improved understanding of relationships between entities.

3. **Example**:

   - o Graph-based positional encodings enhance multi-hop reasoning.

14.2.2 Multi-Modal Fusion

1. **Definition**:

   - o Integrating textual and graph-based inputs in LLMs.

2. **Example**:

   - o Combining natural language descriptions with graph embeddings for richer responses.

3. **Architecture**:

○ Dual encoders for graph embeddings and text, followed by a shared decoder.

14.2.3 Pretraining on Graph-Enriched Data

1. **Overview**:

   ○ Pretraining LLMs on datasets enriched with graph information improves domain-specific performance.

2. **Use Case**:

   ○ Pretraining on a healthcare KG improves medical question-answering accuracy.

3. **Challenges**:

   ○ Balancing graph-based reasoning with general NLP capabilities.

14.2.4 Adaptive Context Windows

1. **Problem**:

   ○ LLMs have fixed context windows, limiting the integration of large graphs.

2. **Solution**:

   ○ Dynamic context windows adapt to include the most relevant graph information.

3. **Example**:

   ○ Summarizing a graph section relevant to a query before feeding it to the LLM.

14.3 AI-Driven Graph Construction and Expansion

14.3.1 Automatic Entity Extraction

1. **Definition**:

    o   Use AI models to extract entities and relationships from unstructured data.

2. **Example**:

    o   Extracting Disease and Symptom entities from medical research papers.

3. **Python Example**:

python

```
from transformers import pipeline

extractor = pipeline("ner", model="dslim/bert-base-NER")
text = "COVID-19 causes fever and cough."
entities = extractor(text)
print(entities)
```

Output:

plaintext

```
[{'entity': 'DISEASE', 'word': 'COVID-19'}, {'entity': 'SYMPTOM',
'word': 'fever'}, {'entity': 'SYMPTOM', 'word': 'cough'}]
```

14.3.2 Relationship Prediction

1. **Definition**:

    o   Use graph neural networks (GNNs) to predict missing relationships in knowledge graphs.

2. **Example**:

    o   Predicting an edge between Disease and Treatment.

Code Example with PyTorch Geometric:

python

```python
import torch
from torch_geometric.nn import GCNConv

class RelationshipPredictor(torch.nn.Module):
    def __init__(self):
        super().__init__()
        self.conv1 = GCNConv(16, 32)
        self.conv2 = GCNConv(32, 16)

    def forward(self, x, edge_index):
        x = self.conv1(x, edge_index).relu()
        x = self.conv2(x, edge_index)
        return x

# Model initialization and edge prediction
```

14.3.3 Graph Augmentation

1. **Overview**:

   o Enrich existing graphs with external data sources.

2. **Example**:

   o Adding real-time financial data to a stock market graph.

14.3.4 Continuous Learning for Graphs

1. **Definition**:

   o AI systems that update graphs dynamically as new data arrives.

2. **Example**:

- A news graph that continuously adds events and relationships.

Implementation Steps:

1. Use web scraping or APIs for data collection.

2. Process data for graph insertion.

3. Automate updates using triggers or pipelines.

14.3.5 Example: Real-Time Graph Expansion

Scenario: A knowledge graph for sports updates with live match data.

Python Example:

python

```python
from neo4j import GraphDatabase

class GraphUpdater:
    def __init__(self, uri, user, password):
        self.driver = GraphDatabase.driver(uri, auth=(user, password))

    def close(self):
        self.driver.close()

    def add_match(self, team1, team2, score):
        query = """
        MERGE (t1:Team {name: $team1})
        MERGE (t2:Team {name: $team2})
        MERGE (m:Match {score: $score})
        MERGE (t1)-[:PLAYED]->(m)-[:PLAYED]->(t2)
        """
        with self.driver.session() as session:
            session.run(query, team1=team1, team2=team2, score=score)
```

```
# Adding a match
updater = GraphUpdater("bolt://localhost:7687", "neo4j", "password")
updater.add_match("Team A", "Team B", "3-2")
updater.close()
```

Summary

1. **Emerging Trends in Knowledge Graphs**:

    o   Hybrid and temporal graphs are becoming central to advanced applications.

2. **LLM Architectures for Graph Integration**:

    o   Enhanced attention mechanisms and multi-modal fusion are driving improvements.

3. **AI-Driven Graph Construction**:

    o   Automation tools for entity extraction, relationship prediction, and graph expansion streamline the creation of robust knowledge graphs.

The next section explores how open knowledge graphs and community contributions will shape the future of AI-driven systems.

Chapter 15: Final Thoughts and Next Steps

This concluding chapter summarizes the key concepts covered in the book, offers resources for continued learning, suggests areas for future research and innovation, and reflects on the broader implications of Graph RAG systems and their potential.

15.1 Key Takeaways from the Book

15.1.1 Understanding Graph RAG

1. **Definition**:
   - Graph RAG integrates knowledge graphs with Retrieval-Augmented Generation (RAG) systems to improve reasoning and contextual accuracy in AI.

2. **Core Components**:
   - **Knowledge Graphs**:
     - Provide structured, relational data.
   - **Large Language Models (LLMs)**:
     - Generate coherent, context-aware responses.

15.1.2 Benefits of Graph RAG

1. **Enhanced Reasoning**:
   - Leverages multi-hop relationships to answer complex queries.

2. **Scalability**:

       o Handles large datasets through graph partitioning and distributed systems.

3. **Flexibility**:

       o Adapts to diverse applications, from healthcare to e-commerce.

15.1.3 Challenges and Solutions

1. **Challenges**:

       o Data noise, computational overhead, and biases.

2. **Solutions**:

       o Use robust graph construction techniques, optimize queries, and implement ethical AI principles.

15.1.4 Real-World Applications

- Explored use cases include:

       o **Healthcare**: Disease diagnosis and treatment recommendations.

       o **Education**: Personalized learning paths.

       o **Legal Research**: Document summarization and case linkage.

15.2 Resources for Continued Learning

15.2.1 Books and Publications

1. **Knowledge Graphs and Semantic Web**:

       o *"Foundations of Semantic Web Technologies"* by Pascal Hitzler, Markus Krötzsch, and Sebastian Rudolph.

2. **Graph Databases**:

   - *"Graph Databases"* by Ian Robinson, Jim Webber, and Emil Eifrem.

3. **Natural Language Processing**:

   - *"Speech and Language Processing"* by Daniel Jurafsky and James H. Martin.

15.2.2 Online Courses

1. **Neo4j Academy**:

   - Free courses on building and querying graph databases.

2. **Coursera**:

   - *Knowledge Graphs for Beginners* by the University of Amsterdam.

3. **edX**:

   - *Introduction to AI* by Columbia University.

15.2.3 Open-Source Tools

1. **Neo4j**:

   - Popular graph database with community and enterprise editions.

2. **RDFLib**:

   - Python library for RDF data and SPARQL queries.

3. **Apache TinkerPop**:

   - A graph computing framework.

15.2.4 Communities and Forums

1. **LinkedIn Groups**:

   o Join communities focused on AI, NLP, and knowledge graphs.

2. **GitHub Repositories**:

   o Explore projects and contribute to open-source Graph RAG implementations.

3. **Stack Overflow**:

   o Engage in technical discussions and seek troubleshooting advice.

15.3 Suggestions for Future Research and Innovation

15.3.1 Advanced Graph Reasoning

1. **Temporal and Spatial Graphs**:

   o Incorporate time and location data for dynamic reasoning.

   o Example: Tracking climate change impacts over decades.

2. **Explainable AI**:

   o Focus on creating transparent reasoning paths for graph-based decisions.

15.3.2 Improved LLM Integration

1. **Pretraining with Graphs**:

   o Enhance LLMs by incorporating graph data during pretraining.

2. **Dynamic Context Windows**:

   o Enable LLMs to process larger graph-based contexts efficiently.

15.3.3 Scalability and Optimization

1. **Distributed Systems**:

   o Research methods for scaling graph databases across cloud infrastructures.

2. **Query Optimization**:

   o Develop algorithms for faster and more efficient graph queries.

15.3.4 Cross-Domain Applications

1. **Healthcare and Genomics**:

   o Expand Graph RAG to support precision medicine and genetic research.

2. **Legal Systems**:

   o Enhance document summarization and case-law research.

15.3.5 Ethics in Graph RAG

1. **Bias Mitigation**:

   o Research algorithms to detect and reduce biases in graph data.

2. **Privacy Preservation**:

   o Develop anonymization techniques for sensitive graph datasets.

15.4 Closing Reflections

15.4.1 The Transformative Potential of Graph RAG

Graph RAG systems are at the forefront of AI innovation, offering unprecedented capabilities for reasoning and knowledge representation. By integrating knowledge graphs with LLMs, these systems provide scalable, accurate, and context-aware solutions across industries.

15.4.2 The Role of Collaboration

1. **Community Contributions**:

   o Open-source tools and knowledge sharing are critical for advancing Graph RAG.

2. **Cross-Industry Collaboration**:

   o Joint efforts among industries, academia, and governments can unlock new applications.

15.4.3 A Call to Action

Readers are encouraged to:

1. **Experiment**:

   o Apply Graph RAG concepts in their projects.

2. **Contribute**:

   o Share insights and collaborate within the AI community.

3. **Innovate**:

- o Explore new ways to integrate and extend Graph RAG systems.

Summary

1. **Key Takeaways**:

   - o Graph RAG combines the strengths of knowledge graphs and LLMs for advanced AI applications.

2. **Learning Resources**:

   - o Books, courses, and tools offer avenues for further exploration.

3. **Future Directions**:

   - o Opportunities abound in reasoning, scalability, ethics, and cross-domain applications.

4. **Reflections**:

   - o The journey with Graph RAG is just beginning, and its potential is limitless.

This book aims to equip you with the knowledge and tools to innovate in the field of Graph RAG. The future of AI is interconnected, and your contributions will shape its trajectory.

Appendices

The appendices provide supplementary resources to enhance your understanding of Graph RAG systems. These sections include a glossary of key terms, frequently used code snippets, and recommendations for tools and resources.

Appendix A: Glossary of Terms

This glossary defines key terms used throughout the book, offering clarity on essential concepts.

Term	Definition
Graph RAG	Retrieval-Augmented Generation powered by knowledge graphs to enhance reasoning and context.
Knowledge Graph (KG)	A structured representation of entities (nodes) and their relationships (edges).
Node	A graph element representing an entity (e.g., a person, place, or object).
Edge	A connection between two nodes, representing their relationship.
SPARQL	A query language for retrieving data stored in RDF format.
Cypher	A declarative query language for interacting with graph databases like Neo4j.
Entity Extraction	Identifying and categorizing entities (e.g., names, dates) in unstructured text.
Multi-Hop Reasoning	The process of connecting multiple graph nodes to infer complex relationships.
Temporal	A knowledge graph with time-based data for

Term	Definition
Graph	dynamic reasoning.
Federated Graph	A distributed graph that integrates data from multiple sources.

Appendix B: Frequently Used Code Snippets

This section provides practical code snippets to streamline your work with Graph RAG systems.

1. Connecting to a Neo4j Database

python

```python
from neo4j import GraphDatabase

class GraphConnection:
    def __init__(self, uri, user, password):
        self.driver = GraphDatabase.driver(uri, auth=(user, password))

    def close(self):
        self.driver.close()

    def run_query(self, query, params={}):
        with self.driver.session() as session:
            return session.run(query, **params)

# Example Usage
conn = GraphConnection("bolt://localhost:7687", "neo4j", "password")
results = conn.run_query("MATCH (n) RETURN n LIMIT 10")
for record in results:
    print(record)
conn.close()
```

2. Querying a Knowledge Graph with SPARQL

python

```python
from SPARQLWrapper import SPARQLWrapper, JSON

def query_sparql(endpoint, sparql_query):
    sparql = SPARQLWrapper(endpoint)
    sparql.setQuery(sparql_query)
    sparql.setReturnFormat(JSON)
    return sparql.query().convert()

# Example Usage
endpoint = "https://query.wikidata.org/sparql"
query = """
SELECT ?country ?population WHERE {
  ?country wdt:P31 wd:Q6256; # Instance of Country
       wdt:P1082 ?population. # Population
}
LIMIT 10
"""
results = query_sparql(endpoint, query)
for result in results["results"]["bindings"]:
    print(result)
```

3. Filtering Noisy Data

python

```python
def filter_noisy_nodes(graph_data, threshold):
    return [node for node in graph_data if node['relevance_score'] >
threshold]
```

```
# Example Usage
nodes = [{"name": "Node1", "relevance_score": 0.9}, {"name": "Node2",
"relevance_score": 0.2}]
filtered_nodes = filter_noisy_nodes(nodes, 0.5)
print(filtered_nodes)
```

Output:

plaintext

```
[{'name': 'Node1', 'relevance_score': 0.9}]
```

4. Entity Extraction with Transformers

python

```
from transformers import pipeline

extractor = pipeline("ner", model="dslim/bert-base-NER")
text = "COVID-19 causes fever and cough."
entities = extractor(text)
print(entities)
```

Output:

plaintext

```
[{'entity': 'DISEASE', 'word': 'COVID-19'}, {'entity': 'SYMPTOM',
'word': 'fever'}, {'entity': 'SYMPTOM', 'word': 'cough'}]
```

5. Creating a Simple Knowledge Graph

cypher

```
CREATE (a:Person {name: 'Alice'})-[:KNOWS]->(b:Person {name:
'Bob'});
```

Appendix C: Recommended Tools and Resources

This appendix lists essential tools and resources for building and managing Graph RAG systems.

1. Graph Databases

- **Neo4j**:
    - Features: Cypher query language, visualization tools, scalability.
    - Website: neo4j.com
- **Amazon Neptune**:
    - Features: Fully managed graph database with RDF and Gremlin support.
    - Website: aws.amazon.com/neptune
- **ArangoDB**:
    - Features: Multi-model database with graph, document, and key/value capabilities.
    - Website: arangodb.com

2. Query Languages

- **SPARQL**:
    - Use: Query RDF-based knowledge graphs.
    - Documentation: w3.org/TR/sparql11-query/
- **Cypher**:

- o Use: Query Neo4j databases.
- o Documentation: neo4j.com/docs/cypher-manual/

---

3. Open Knowledge Graphs

- **Wikidata**:
  - o Description: Free and open knowledge base for structured data.
  - o Website: wikidata.org
- **DBpedia**:
  - o Description: Knowledge graph extracted from Wikipedia.
  - o Website: dbpedia.org

---

4. Machine Learning Libraries

- **PyTorch Geometric**:
  - o Features: Tools for building and training graph neural networks.
  - o Website: pytorch-geometric.readthedocs.io
- **DGL (Deep Graph Library)**:
  - o Features: Scalable framework for graph-based machine learning.
  - o Website: dgl.ai

---

5. Visualization Tools

- **Gephi**:
  - o Features: Open-source platform for graph visualization and analysis.

- Website: gephi.org
- **Neo4j Bloom**:
    - Features: Interactive graph visualization for Neo4j.
    - Website: neo4j.com/bloom

---

6. Educational Resources

- **Neo4j Academy**:
    - Free courses on Neo4j and graph database concepts.
    - Website: neo4j.com/graphacademy/
- **Stanford Graph Learning**:
    - Online lectures on graph theory and neural networks.
    - Website: cs.stanford.edu

Summary

1. **Glossary of Terms**:
    - Definitions of key terms to clarify foundational concepts.
2. **Code Snippets**:
    - Practical examples for tasks like querying and graph construction.
3. **Recommended Tools**:
    - Comprehensive list of databases, libraries, and visualization platforms.

These appendices aim to be your quick reference for diving deeper into Graph RAG systems and their practical implementations.

Appendix D: Practice Datasets for Knowledge Graphs

This appendix provides a curated list of practice datasets suitable for building, querying, and experimenting with knowledge graphs. These datasets span various domains, including open datasets for public use and specialized collections for advanced applications.

D.1 General Knowledge Datasets

1. **Wikidata**

    o **Description**: A collaborative, open-source knowledge base with millions of structured entities and relationships.

    o **Use Cases**: Entity linking, fact retrieval, and relationship discovery.

    o **Access**: wikidata.org

    o **Sample Query** (SPARQL):

sparql

```
SELECT ?person ?birthPlace WHERE {
  ?person wdt:P31 wd:Q5; # Instance of human
      wdt:P19 ?birthPlace. # Birthplace
}
LIMIT 10
```

2. **DBpedia**

    o **Description**: Structured data extracted from Wikipedia, covering a wide range of topics.

    o **Use Cases**: Semantic search, ontology learning, and knowledge graph enrichment.

    o **Access**: dbpedia.org

3. **Freebase**

- Description: A large collaborative knowledge base containing structured data across diverse domains.

- Use Cases: Knowledge base augmentation and semantic reasoning.

- Access: archive.org

D.2 Domain-Specific Datasets

1. **Healthcare**

   - **MIMIC-III**

     - Description: Medical information dataset for ICU patients, including relationships between diagnoses, treatments, and outcomes.

     - Access: physionet.org

     - Use Case: Building medical knowledge graphs for disease diagnosis.

   - **Snomed CT**

     - Description: A comprehensive clinical terminology dataset.

     - Access: snomed.org

2. **Finance**

   - **World Bank Open Data**

     - Description: Comprehensive financial and economic data across countries.

     - Access: data.worldbank.org

     - Use Case: Financial forecasting and risk analysis using graph-based reasoning.

3. **Science and Research**

   - **Microsoft Academic Graph (MAG)**

- Description: A dataset containing academic papers, authors, and their relationships.
- Access: microsoft.com
- Use Case: Building a citation knowledge graph.

4. **Geospatial**

   o **OpenStreetMap**

      - Description: A detailed open-source map dataset with geospatial relationships.
      - Access: openstreetmap.org

D.3 Synthetic Datasets

- **Graph Benchmark Datasets**:
   o Generated datasets for testing graph algorithms and scalability.
   o Examples:
      - **LDBC Social Network Benchmark**: ldbcouncil.org
      - **OGB (Open Graph Benchmark)**: ogb.stanford.edu

D.4 Dataset Preparation

- To prepare and integrate datasets into knowledge graphs:
   1. **Data Cleaning**: Remove noise and standardize formats.
   2. **Schema Mapping**: Define graph nodes and edges based on dataset attributes.

3. **Data Loading**: Use tools like Neo4j's ETL or RDFLib for importing data.

Example Python Code for Data Loading:

python

```
from neo4j import GraphDatabase

class DataLoader:
    def __init__(self, uri, user, password):
        self.driver = GraphDatabase.driver(uri, auth=(user, password))

    def close(self):
        self.driver.close()

    def load_data(self, data):
        query = """
        UNWIND $data AS row
        MERGE (entity:Entity {name: row.name})
        """
        with self.driver.session() as session:
            session.run(query, data=data)

# Load sample data
data = [{"name": "Entity1"}, {"name": "Entity2"}]
loader = DataLoader("bolt://localhost:7687", "neo4j", "password")
loader.load_data(data)
loader.close()
```

Appendix E: Solutions to Chapter Exercises

This section provides solutions to the exercises presented at the end of each chapter. These solutions are designed to reinforce learning and provide a reference for self-assessment.

E.1 Example from Chapter 7: Graph Traversal

Problem: Query a knowledge graph to find diseases related to a symptom.
Solution:

cypher

```
MATCH (s:Symptom {name: "Fever"})-[:HAS_SYMPTOM]-
>(d:Disease)
RETURN d.name
```

Expected Output:

Disease Name

Influenza

Malaria

E.2 Example from Chapter 8: Combining Graph Data with LLMs

Problem: Integrate graph data with an LLM to generate a response.
Solution:

python

```
from transformers import pipeline

# Graph query result
context = "The disease Malaria is caused by Plasmodium parasites and
transmitted by mosquitoes."

# LLM Integration
generator = pipeline("text-generation", model="gpt-3.5")
```

```
prompt = f"Explain the context: {context}"
response = generator(prompt, max_length=100)
print(response[0]["generated_text"])
```

Expected Output:

plaintext

Malaria is caused by Plasmodium parasites, which are transmitted to humans through the bites of infected mosquitoes. Effective treatment is available.

E.3 Example from Chapter 12: Debugging and Optimization

Problem: Optimize a graph query to retrieve top products.
Solution:

cypher

```
MATCH (u:User {name: "Alice"})-[:PURCHASED]->(p:Product)-
[:SIMILAR_TO]->(rec:Product)
WHERE rec.price < 100
RETURN rec.name
LIMIT 5
```

Expected Output:

Product Name

Product A

Product B

Summary

   1. **Practice Datasets**:

o   A variety of open and domain-specific datasets to build and experiment with knowledge graphs.

2. **Solutions to Exercises**:

o   Detailed solutions to reinforce learning and improve problem-solving skills.

These appendices provide comprehensive support for applying the concepts learned in this book, ensuring practical, hands-on experience with Graph RAG systems.

References

This section provides an extensive list of resources, including research papers, books, articles, and open-source tools, to deepen your understanding of LLMs (Large Language Models), Knowledge Graphs, and Retrieval-Augmented Generation (RAG). These references are carefully curated to serve as a foundation for continued learning and practical application.

A. Research Papers on LLMs, Knowledge Graphs, and RAG

1. **Large Language Models**

   - *Attention Is All You Need*

     - Authors: Vaswani et al.

     - Published: 2017

     - Description: Introduced the Transformer architecture, the backbone of modern LLMs.

     - Link: arxiv.org/abs/1706.03762

   - *Language Models Are Few-Shot Learners*

     - Authors: Brown et al.

     - Published: 2020

     - Description: Introduced GPT-3, demonstrating the capabilities of LLMs for various NLP tasks.

     - Link: arxiv.org/abs/2005.14165

2. **Knowledge Graphs**

   - *A Survey of Knowledge Graph Embedding Techniques*

     - Authors: Ji et al.

     - Published: 2021

- Description: Comprehensive review of techniques for embedding knowledge graphs.
- Link: arxiv.org/abs/2002.00388

o *Knowledge Graph Completion with Transformers*

- Authors: Wang et al.
- Published: 2022
- Description: Explores Transformer-based approaches for graph completion tasks.
- Link: arxiv.org/abs/2204.06676

3. **Retrieval-Augmented Generation (RAG)**

o *RAG: Retrieval-Augmented Generation for Knowledge-Intensive NLP Tasks*

- Authors: Lewis et al.
- Published: 2020
- Description: Presents RAG, combining retrieval systems with generative models for knowledge-intensive tasks.
- Link: arxiv.org/abs/2005.11401

o *Dense Passage Retrieval for Open-Domain Question Answering*

- Authors: Karpukhin et al.
- Published: 2020
- Description: Discusses Dense Passage Retrieval (DPR), an efficient retriever for RAG systems.
- Link: arxiv.org/abs/2004.04906

B. Books and Articles on AI and Graph Theory

B.1 Foundational Books

1. **Deep Learning**
   - Authors: Ian Goodfellow, Yoshua Bengio, and Aaron Courville
   - Published: 2016
   - Description: Comprehensive introduction to deep learning concepts, including neural networks and applications.
   - Link: deeplearningbook.org

2. **Graph Databases: New Opportunities for Connected Data**
   - Authors: Ian Robinson, Jim Webber, and Emil Eifrem
   - Published: 2015
   - Description: Detailed exploration of graph databases and their applications in modern data science.
   - Link: neo4j.com/books/graph-databases

3. **Hands-On Graph Analytics with Neo4j**
   - Authors: Estelle Scifo
   - Published: 2020
   - Description: Practical guide to graph analytics using Neo4j with real-world examples.

4. **Foundations of Semantic Web Technologies**
   - Authors: Pascal Hitzler, Markus Krötzsch, and Sebastian Rudolph
   - Published: 2010
   - Description: Covers RDF, OWL, and SPARQL, essential for building semantic knowledge graphs.

B.2 Articles and Tutorials

1. *Exploring Knowledge Graphs with SPARQL*

   o Published by: Neo4j Blog

   o Description: Step-by-step tutorial for querying and analyzing knowledge graphs using SPARQL.

   o Link: neo4j.com/blog

2. *Introduction to Transformers*

   o Published by: Hugging Face Blog

   o Description: In-depth guide to Transformer models and their role in NLP.

   o Link: huggingface.co/blog

3. *Building Scalable Knowledge Graphs*

   o Published by: Towards Data Science

   o Description: Explains techniques for constructing and scaling knowledge graphs.

   o Link: towardsdatascience.com

C. Open-Source Tools and Libraries

C.1 Graph Databases

1. **Neo4j**

   o Description: Popular graph database for building and querying large-scale knowledge graphs.

   o Features: Cypher query language, high scalability.

   o Website: neo4j.com

2. **ArangoDB**

   o Description: Multi-model database supporting graph, document, and key-value storage.

   o Website: arangodb.com

3. **Amazon Neptune**

   o Description: Fully managed graph database with support for RDF and Gremlin.

   o Website: aws.amazon.com/neptune

C.2 Machine Learning Libraries

1. **PyTorch Geometric**

   o Description: Framework for building graph neural networks and advanced graph analytics.

   o Website: pytorch-geometric.readthedocs.io

2. **DGL (Deep Graph Library)**

   o Description: Scalable graph processing library for building graph-based models.

   o Website: dgl.ai

C.3 Visualization Tools

1. **Gephi**

   o Description: Open-source platform for graph visualization and analysis.

   o Website: gephi.org

2. **Neo4j Bloom**

   o Description: Interactive visualization tool for exploring Neo4j graphs.

   o Website: neo4j.com/bloom

C.4 NLP Libraries

1. **Hugging Face Transformers**

- o Description: Library for working with Transformer-based models.

- o Website: huggingface.co

2. **spaCy**

- o Description: NLP library with support for entity extraction and knowledge graph construction.

- o Website: spacy.io

C.5 Query Languages and APIs

1. **SPARQL**

- o Description: Query language for RDF-based knowledge graphs.

- o Documentation: w3.org/TR/sparql11-query/

2. **Cypher**

- o Description: Declarative query language for Neo4j.

- o Documentation: neo4j.com/docs/cypher-manual/

Summary

1. **Research Papers**:

- o Foundational studies on LLMs, knowledge graphs, and RAG systems.

2. **Books and Articles**:

- o Comprehensive resources for understanding graph theory and AI concepts.

3. **Open-Source Tools**:

- o Libraries and platforms to build, query, and analyze Graph RAG systems.

These references provide a robust foundation for readers to expand their knowledge and apply concepts in real-world scenarios.

You said:

Index An exhaustive index for quick reference to key terms and concepts. Write in details and exhaustively on this informatively, using a full length,clear, simple style of writing keeping the language basic and professional. Always ensure all tables, code examples are complete, accurate and well explained

ChatGPT said:

ChatGPT

Index

This exhaustive index provides a quick reference to key terms, concepts, tools, and topics discussed throughout the book. Organized alphabetically, it allows readers to navigate the content efficiently and revisit important sections with ease.

A

- **AI-Driven Graph Construction**:
  Explanation of automated graph-building techniques using machine learning. See *Chapter 14.3*.
  Tools: PyTorch Geometric, RDFLib.

- **ArangoDB**:
  Multi-model database supporting graph operations. See *Appendix C.1*.
  Website: arangodb.com.

- **Attention Mechanisms**:
  Enhanced Transformer components for graph-based reasoning. See *Chapter 14.2.1*.

B

- **Bias in Knowledge Graphs**:
  Addressing fairness and ethical considerations in graph data.
  See *Chapter 11.2*.
  Solutions: Weight adjustments, diverse data sources.

- **Bloom, Neo4j**:
  Interactive visualization tool for Neo4j graphs. See *Appendix C.3*.
  Website: neo4j.com/bloom.

- **Books on AI and Graph Theory**:
  Comprehensive list of recommended readings. See *Appendix B.1*.
  Examples: *Graph Databases* by Ian Robinson, *Deep Learning* by Ian Goodfellow.

C

- **Cypher Query Language**:
  Declarative query language for Neo4j databases. See *Chapter 5.3* and *Appendix C.5*.
  Example Query:

cypher

```
MATCH (n:Node)-[:RELATES_TO]->(m:Node)

RETURN n, m
```

- **Community Contributions**:
  Role of open-source projects in advancing Graph RAG. See *Chapter 13.5*.
  Examples: Wikidata, DBpedia.

- **Cross-Industry Collaboration**:
  Sharing knowledge graphs between domains for innovation.
  See *Chapter 13.4*.
  Examples: Healthcare and AI partnerships.

D

- **Data Noise**:
  Techniques for identifying and removing noisy or irrelevant data. See *Chapter 12.2*.
  Code Example: Filtering noisy nodes in Python.

- **Dataset Preparation**:
  Steps for cleaning, structuring, and integrating data into graphs. See *Appendix D.4*.
  Tools: Neo4j ETL, RDFLib.

E

- **Entity Extraction**:
  Identifying and categorizing entities in unstructured data. See *Chapter 14.3.1*.
  Example Tool: Hugging Face Transformers.
  Code Snippet:

python

```
from transformers import pipeline

extractor = pipeline("ner", model="dslim/bert-base-NER")
```

- **Ethics in AI**:
  Addressing privacy, bias, and transparency in Graph RAG. See *Chapter 11.4*.
  Examples: Bias mitigation in healthcare graphs.

F

- **Federated Knowledge Graphs**:
  Distributed graphs integrating data from multiple sources. See *Chapter 14.1.4*.
  Challenges: Data harmonization, security.

- **Freebase**:
  Open-source knowledge base for diverse domains. See *Appendix D.1*.
  Access: archive.org.

G

- **Gephi**:
  Open-source tool for graph visualization and analysis. See *Appendix C.3*.
  Website: gephi.org.

- **Graph Neural Networks (GNNs)**:
  Advanced reasoning with graph-based machine learning models. See *Chapter 9.3*.
  Tools: PyTorch Geometric, DGL.

H

- **Healthcare Applications**:
  Use of Graph RAG for disease diagnosis and personalized medicine. See *Chapter 10.2*.
  Example Graph: Disease-Symptom relationships.

- **Hybrid Knowledge Graphs**:
  Combining symbolic graphs with neural embeddings. See *Chapter 14.1.1*.

I

- **Indexing in Graph Databases**:
  Techniques for optimizing query performance. See *Chapter 12.3.2*.
  Example Query:

cypher

CREATE INDEX ON :Node(attribute)

K

- **Knowledge Graphs**:
  Structured data representation with nodes and edges. See *Chapter 4.1*.
  Types: Ontological, taxonomical, temporal.
  Tools: Neo4j, RDFLib.

L

- **LLM Architectures**:
  Advances in integrating large language models with knowledge graphs. See *Chapter 14.2*.
  Techniques: Multi-modal fusion, adaptive context windows.

- **Limitations of LLMs**:
  Addressing the inability to access external knowledge natively. See *Chapter 2.4*.
  Solutions: Retrieval-Augmented Generation (RAG).

M

- **Microsoft Academic Graph (MAG)**:
  Dataset linking academic papers and authors. See *Appendix D.2*.
  Use Case: Citation analysis and graph-based research.

- **Multi-Hop Reasoning**:
  Connecting multiple graph nodes for complex queries. See *Chapter 7.4*.
  Example Query: Finding diseases linked to multiple symptoms.

N

- **Neo4j**:
  Popular graph database for building and querying knowledge graphs. See *Chapter 5.2*.
  Features: Cypher language, scalability.
  Website: neo4j.com.

O

- **Open Knowledge Graphs**:
  Publicly accessible datasets like Wikidata and DBpedia. See *Appendix D.1*.
  Applications: Semantic search, recommendation systems.

P

- **Practice Datasets**:
  Recommended datasets for building and experimenting with graphs. See *Appendix D*.
  Examples: MIMIC-III (Healthcare), OpenStreetMap (Geospatial).

R

- **RAG Systems**:
  Retrieval-Augmented Generation systems for contextual knowledge retrieval. See *Chapter 1.2*.
  Papers: *RAG: Retrieval-Augmented Generation for Knowledge-Intensive NLP Tasks*.

- **RDFLib**:
  Python library for creating and querying RDF-based graphs. See *Appendix C.2*.
  Example Use: SPARQL query execution.

S

- **SPARQL**:
  Query language for RDF knowledge graphs. See *Appendix C.5*.
  Example Query:

sparql

```
SELECT ?subject ?predicate ?object WHERE {

  ?subject ?predicate ?object.

}
```

T

- **Temporal Graphs**:
  Knowledge graphs incorporating time-based relationships. See *Chapter 14.1.2*.
  Example: Tracking financial trends over time.

V

- **Visualization Tools**:
  Tools for exploring and analyzing graph data. See *Appendix C.3*.
  Examples: Gephi, Neo4j Bloom.

Summary

This index provides an extensive, organized reference to all key terms and concepts in the book. Use it to quickly locate discussions on specific topics, revisit critical examples, or dive deeper into practical applications of Graph RAG systems.